THE CANDIDATE

ALSO BY PAUL ALEXANDER

Man of the People: The Life of John McCain
Salinger: A Biography
*Death and Disaster: The Rise of the Warhol Empire
and the Race for Andy's Millions*
*Boulevard of Broken Dreams:
The Life, Times, and Legend of James Dean*
Rough Magic: A Biography of Sylvia Plath
Ariel Ascending: Writings About Sylvia Plath (Editor)

PLAYS

Edge
Strangers in the Land of Canaan

THE CANDIDATE

*Behind John Kerry's Remarkable
Run for the White House*

PAUL ALEXANDER

RIVERHEAD BOOKS
a member of
Penguin Group (USA) Inc.
New York
2004

Riverhead Books
a member of
Penguin Group (USA) Inc.
375 Hudson Street
New York, NY 10014

Library of Congress Cataloging-in-Publication Data

Alexander, Paul, date.
The candidate : behind John Kerry's remarkable run for the White House /
by Paul Alexander.
p. cm.
ISBN 1-57322-293-3
1. John Kerry, 1943–   2. Presidents—United States—Election—2004.
3. Political campaigns—United States.   4. Presidential candidates—United
States—Biography.   5. Legislators—United States—Biography.
6. United States. Congress. Senate—Biography.   I. Title.
E840.8.K427A44   2004   2004050755
973.931'092—dc22

Printed in the United States of America
1   3   5   7   9   10   8   6   4   2

This book is printed on acid-free paper. ∞

Book design by Stephanie Huntwork

For Lauren, as always
For my family
And for Iris Gordon Rossi

CONTENTS

THE CANDIDATE

We made a promise we swore we'd always remember
No retreat, no surrender . . .
Blood brothers in a stormy night with a vow to defend
No retreat, no surrender

—BRUCE SPRINGSTEEN

"No Surrender"

1

"MISSION ACCOMPLISHED!"

The S-3B Viking jet descended from the cobalt-blue sky at somewhere between 125 and 150 miles per hour and approached the flight deck of the USS *Abraham Lincoln*. On its way home to Everett, Washington, after an almost ten-month-long tour of duty as part of the operations in Iraq, the aircraft carrier was positioned in the Pacific Ocean thirty miles off the coast of California near San Diego. The pilot of the snub-nosed, 53-foot-long four-seater, Commander John Lussier—a "mature" flyer, to quote a navy colleague—was known for his smooth landings. Carefully, Lussier guided the jet in its descent until it touched down, still zooming ahead at full speed, onto the flight deck, catching its tailhook on a metal cable stretched across the deck and coming to a dead stop so abruptly that it produced a g-force twice that of gravity. The local time at touchdown was 12:16 P.M. The date was May 1, 2003.

Today's flight was no ordinary mission. There were clues to its unique status on the aircraft itself. NAVY 1 was painted on its rear. Just underneath the cockpit window, GEORGE W. BUSH, COMMANDER-IN-CHIEF was painted in script. The two seats behind Lussier were occupied by a Secret Service agent and a spare pilot, and sitting beside Lussier in the copilot seat was the President of the United States himself, dressed in a regulation flight suit topped off with a white helmet. Earlier in the day, Bush had flown on *Air Force One* from Washington, D.C., to the Naval Air Station North Island in San Diego, where he had replaced his civilian clothes with the green flight suit, undergone training for a possible emergency landing on water, and boarded the Viking jet that would fly him from San Diego to the *Abraham Lincoln.* According to press reports, Bush, a trained pilot who had served in the Texas Air National Guard in the Vietnam era, flew the jet himself for about one-third of the trip. This could have been why he appeared exuberant and confident as he climbed out of the cockpit and jumped down onto the deck, helmet tucked under one arm. The image was striking. The moment was historic. It was the first time a sitting president had flown in a jet that landed on an aircraft carrier.

Bush shook hands with the sailors who approached him on the flight deck. "Thank you," he would say, or " 'preciate it." When a group of reporters asked if he had flown the jet himself, he answered, "Yes, I flew it. Yeah, of course, I liked it." Before long, crewmen were posing for pictures with Bush, who gladly complied, often throwing one arm around the sailor's shoulder or slapping him on the back. "Good job," Bush said, smiling broadly. He meant, one must presume, the crew's participation in the military operations in Iraq. For, hovering above the scene as it was broadcast live on television—a shot that would be replayed on the news that evening and in the days and weeks to come—was a massive banner that read MISSION ACCOMPLISHED!

That night, at 9:00 P.M. Eastern time, Bush was on television again, this time to deliver a speech that marked the end of principal military action in Iraq. Dressed in civilian clothes, Bush stood at a podium and spoke to an audience of officers and crewmen from the *Abraham Lincoln,* who often interrupted him with applause. "Major combat operations in Iraq have ended," Bush announced. "In the battle of Iraq, the United States and our allies have prevailed." Applause! Listing those allies as the United Kingdom, Australia, and Poland, Bush thanked the Iraqi citizens "who welcomed our troops and joined in the liberation of their own country" before he declared: "We've begun the search for hidden chemical and biological weapons, and already know of hundreds of sites that will be investigated. . . . And we will stand with the new leaders of Iraq as they establish a government of, by, and for the Iraqi people." Applause! Then he added: "We have removed an ally of al Qaeda and cut off a source of terrorist funding. And this much is certain: no terrorist network will gain weapons of mass destruction from the Iraqi regime, because the regime is no more." Applause! Finally, Bush summed up the Iraqi mission with a quote from the prophet Isaiah: "To the captives, come out; and to those in darkness, be free."

The speech stood as a remarkable moment in the Bush presidency—and was more than slightly ironic, given future developments—but the event of May 1 that would remain truly memorable was Bush's tailhook landing on the aircraft carrier. In his office in the White House, Vice President Dick Cheney watched the landing on television and, as it was later reported, could not help but break into a big smile, according to an aide. Many in the Republican Party were pleased that day. Bush enthusiasts agreed that the tailhook landing was a spectacular piece of presidential theater. "There he was, slapping officers on the back, posing for pictures, joking with sailors and aviators," journalist Gleaves Whitney would write in the *National Review* a week later. "You can bet your bottom dollar these images will be used during the 2004 campaign—they'll make Bush harder to beat."

In his office in the Russell Building, John Kerry, the senator from Massachusetts who was seeking the Democratic presidential nomination, could hardly believe what he was seeing. "This is amazing," he said to no one in particular as he and members of his staff watched the landing.

When Bush got out of the cockpit and walked underneath the MISSION ACCOMPLISHED! sign, Kerry decided that the event, so clearly staged for the media, represented a shocking example of hubris. Kerry didn't have a problem with Bush thanking the troops for what they had gone through in Iraq. In the late 1960s, Kerry himself had been a young member of the American military fighting a war thousands of miles away from the homeland. So Kerry understood—even appreciated—the importance of Bush's gesture: it is appropriate for a president, the commander in chief, to recognize the efforts of his troops after a successful conflict. What offended Kerry was Bush's willingness to make himself—as opposed to the troops—the center of attention. That took a kind of arrogance to which a seasoned military officer would never succumb. Any officer worth respect knows that the troops themselves, not the officers, deserve all of the praise.

While Kerry sat in his office that day, his aides coming and going as the television played, he resolved to keep his feelings private. It would be inappropriate, he concluded, to release a statement or make comments to the press that were critical of Bush. If he were to go public and call Bush's landing on the aircraft carrier what it was—a publicity stunt—it would only serve to distract from Bush's thanking of the troops. So he would keep quiet.

As the rest of the afternoon passed, Kerry could not help but remember how differently the nation had treated the Vietnam veterans, of which he was one, when they returned home in the late 1960s and early 1970s. There were no parades, no marching bands, no welcome-home celebrations. President Nixon did not seize the media spotlight, on the deck of an aircraft carrier or anywhere else, to thank the troops for what they had gone through in Southeast Asia. Even so, for reasons of his own, Kerry decided to let Bush have his fleeting flash of glory, miscalculated as it was, and remain silent about it.

Two days later, however, Kerry was in South Carolina at an event honoring veterans. In the middle of the proceedings, a veteran stood up and addressed Kerry. "You're the only guy running for president," he said, "who doesn't need to play dress-up to know what this war is all about." Kerry understood what the man meant, but he focused on the word choice—*play dress-up.* There was the opinion in some ranks of the American military that Bush, who in 1968 had chosen to join the National Guard instead of answering the draft—the Guard commonly seen at that time as the organization one entered to avoid military service—did not have the training, the experience, or the credentials to call himself a veteran, much less the commander in chief.

Kerry filed away the phrase—*play dress-up*—to be used at a later time.

A little more than two months later, on July 2, President Bush had just finished making a policy announcement in the Roosevelt Room of the White House when he decided to take questions from reporters. In the weeks since he had given his "Mission Accomplished" speech on the deck of the *Abraham Lincoln,* the formal military action in Iraq may have come to a halt, but the killing of U.S.

servicemen had not. Since May 1, according to information released by the Pentagon, more than twenty servicemen had been killed due to "hostile" fire. The attacks were being executed, the Bush Administration said, by Iraqi militants. Only yesterday Bush had said that the rebuilding of Iraq would be a "massive and long-term undertaking," meaning that, regardless of the deadly strikes being carried out— no matter *who* the attackers were—the United States would not pull troops out of Iraq in the foreseeable future.

So now, having agreed to speak with reporters after making an announcement concerning efforts to fight AIDS in Africa, Bush suspected that he might be asked about his resolve to keep troops in Iraq in the face of an ongoing series of guerrilla attacks. When the first question about those attacks came, he was clearly prepared: "Anybody who wants to harm American troops will be found and brought to justice," Bush said. "There are some that feel like if they attack us that we may decide to leave prematurely. They don't understand what they are talking about if that is the case." When reporters interrupted, Bush cut them off. "Let me finish," he said. Then he delivered the line he had readied for the occasion. "There are some," he said, "who feel like the conditions are such that they can attack us there. My answer is, bring 'em on. We have the force necessary to deal with the situation."

Hundreds of miles away, in Manchester, New Hampshire, John Kerry was riding in a minivan from one campaign event to another when he heard news of Bush's taunting of the Iraqi militants. As he sat in the van, his tall frame squeezed into the cramped backseat, he was flabbergasted. "No one who has ever seen combat would say something like that when our kids are in danger," he said to the aides traveling with him. "It's disrespectful to the troops. McCain and Hagel would never say anything like that." Kerry was referring, of course, to Senator John McCain of Arizona and Senator Chuck Hagel of Nebraska, both Republicans, both Vietnam veterans. Kerry finally got so mad that he took out his cell phone and called Max Cleland, the former Democratic senator from Georgia and Vietnam veteran who, one day in April of 1968, had lost an arm and both legs in an explosion while conducting a reconnaissance mission. "It wasn't just reckless or irresponsible for Bush to do what he did," Kerry fumed to Cleland on the phone. "It was just plain wrong."

That night, while taking questions from reporters, Kerry tried to raise the topic of Bush's remarks. But the reporters weren't interested in what he had to say about Bush. Every question dealt with Howard Dean, the former governor of Vermont who was now in the process of eclipsing Kerry as the frontrunner for the Democratic presidential nomination. One reporter even suggested that Kerry's outrage over Bush's comments might just be a ploy to make himself look more like the "angry man," the persona Dean had used to catapult himself to the front of the Democratic pack. Kerry was unable to explain to the reporters—maybe he didn't even try very hard—that his anger at George W. Bush had absolutely nothing to do with Howard Dean. Members of the press corps would have to figure that out on their own in the months ahead.

2

"BRING IT ON!"

The landscape in Iowa is as flat as a dime. In summer, the many pastures and gardens turn much of the land a lush green, but in winter, that same land becomes a brittle brown, until the snow comes to cover it with a white blanket that often stays for months. Regardless of the season, the land is so flat that when driving down a road you can often see your destination miles ahead in the distance, hovering there, waiting for you to arrive. At night, the sky weighs heavy on the horizon, its vastness making each town in the state's litany of towns appear even smaller than it is.

In many ways, Iowa is a throwback to another place and time. Citizens here take pride in their love of country, family, and religion. They celebrate life's simple pleasures—a good day's harvest, a high school basketball game on Friday night, church on Sunday morning. With 91 percent of its land devoted to agriculture, Iowa is dominated by rural life, although these days the villages that dot the countryside tend to feature strip malls and Levittown-like subdivisions of cookie-cutter homes, vintage 1992. Even so, the largest city, Des Moines, has a population of only about 200,000. The state's citizenry, it must also be said, is almost all white. Historically, the population has been about three percent African-American and another three percent Hispanic. So it may seem odd in the larger context of American history that every four years, in contemporary times at least, the national presidential election cycle has started in the middle of winter on the flat plains of Iowa—a state in which the vast majority of the people are Caucasian, the day-to-day life is agrarian, and one of the best-known landmarks is the Amana Colonies, home of the Amish.

On this day—Saturday, November 15, 2003—John Kerry had come to Des Moines, the state's capital, to speak at the Jefferson Jackson Dinner in the Veterans Memorial Auditorium. That morning, he had gotten up early to play hockey with a team of firefighters in West Des Moines. On his way to the game, he gave an interview to Tom Beaumont, a young political reporter with the *Des Moines Register*, to tell him that, despite his fall from frontrunner status, he was in the race to win. Later, in the hockey game, Kerry scored twice. Afterward, he joked with reporters that he hoped tonight's speech would give him a hat trick. Then Kerry showered, packed up his hockey gear, and headed back to the hotel.

He spent much of the rest of the day holed up with his aides in Room 1046, the presidential suite of the Hotel Fort Des Moines, where he was working on the speech he would give that night. He ordered lunch delivered to the suite and huddled with a small clique of staffers, among them John Norris, his state campaign chairman for Iowa; David Wade, his press secretary; Andrei Cherny, his speechwriter; and Marvin Nicholson, the tall, well-mannered, and handsome man who followed Kerry so closely so much of the time that he seemed to be his shadow. In fact, he was his personal aide.

Tonight's event, hosted by the Democratic Party of Iowa as a way to raise an expected $300,000 to pay for its caucuses in January, featured two ground rules that could not be broken: first, each candidate would be allowed to speak for eight minutes—not a moment longer. To make sure that the speaker stayed within the limit, the event coordinators were going to shut off the microphone exactly when a stopwatch hit the eight-minute mark. Second, each candidate had to speak with no prepared text in front of him. As Kerry paced the hotel room, he worked not only at timing out the speech but also at memorizing it. He had decided to debut a new stump speech tonight before the partisan crowd of 8,000 to 10,000 Iowa Democrats.

As Kerry and his aides worked, Wade e-mailed out sections of the speech to some of the 200 reporters who had come to Des Moines from around the country—indeed, the world—to cover the dinner. As Wade got responses from reporters, many asked the same questions: Why wasn't Kerry attacking Howard Dean, the frontrunner? Why wasn't Kerry trying to take Dean out? But Kerry had made a decision: he was *not* going to go after Dean. Instead, he would make George W. Bush his target. From talking to voters over the past weeks, Kerry had concluded that Iowans were searching for a candidate who could defeat Bush in the fall election, not one who wanted to win so badly that he would rip apart another Democrat.

"So if George Bush wants a debate on national security," Kerry said, practicing, his voice hoarse from months of overuse, "I have three words for him I'm sure he will understand. . . ." With his suit jacket off, Kerry looked even taller than he was. Lean despite his penchant for lunches of Burger King Whoppers and french fries, at six feet four inches, he was decidedly Lincolnesque. Over and over, Kerry delivered passages of the speech until he had perfected both the timing and the delivery. He worried about staying within the eight-minute limit. The last thing he needed, given the persistent criticism leveled at him that he tended to drone on too long when he spoke, was to have his microphone shut off in mid-sentence. He couldn't make such an embarrassing blunder, for this speech was too important. It was, Kerry had come to hope this week, the moment that could change the direction of his failing campaign.

These were anxious days for Kerry. After Al Gore, the nominee in 2000, had announced in mid-December 2002 that he would not run in 2004, Kerry had become the presumed frontrunner in early 2003 simply because he was *in* the race. Then, over the summer, Kerry, a star in the United States Senate for almost two decades and a protégé of Ted Kennedy, one of the Senate's lions, had watched his support evaporate as a result of the rival campaign of former Vermont governor Howard Dean. Dean had savvily courted the national media with his much-ballyhooed Sleepless Summer Tour in August 2003, a month that saw Dean's face appear on the covers of *Time* and *Newsweek* simultaneously—a feat that only a few politicians had ever pulled off. Because of this worshipful press coverage, Dean was soon playing to huge and enthusiastic crowds across the country—in Seattle; New York City; Madison, Wisconsin—even as he mounted what would become an historic Internet-driven fund-raising operation that eventually generated more than $50 million in contributions from some 319,000 donors. No politician had ever utilized the Internet to raise such a staggering sum. Dean would try to use that war chest, in effect, to buy the nomination. He intended to start that process by winning the Iowa caucus in January.

The Dean campaign was being run by an energetic, maverick political guru named Joe Trippi and featured such political novices as

Zephyr Teachout—the smart and upbeat child of 1960s flower children—who had helped define the way the campaign had made use of the Internet. The Dean campaign had broken through in mid- to late summer, thanks in large part to unparalleled media attention (Dean would also be given cover stories by *U.S. News and World Report, The Economist, The New Republic, The Weekly Standard,* and *The Nation,* to name a few), and as Dean solidified his position as frontrunner, Kerry sank in the polls. By summer's end, Kerry was sliding badly. By September, when he officially declared his candidacy for president on a four-state announcement tour, the media, still agog over Dean and his sleepless summer, dismissed Kerry as a Washington stiff whose campaign seemed more a personal indulgence than a serious attempt at becoming his party's nominee.

The media had made its determination: Dean was the story; he had dared to attack Bush on the issue of the war in Iraq when no one else would and, in so doing, had connected with voters. He had also picked up key endorsements from groups like the Service Employees International and the American Federation of State, County, and Municipal Employees. Consequently, Kerry was labeled just another blowhard senator running for president who didn't stand a chance. He even *talked* like a senator. Dean, on the other hand, spoke a language ordinary people understood. Sometimes he was angry, sometimes he was tactless, but his anger and bluntness were symptoms of how he felt about Bush and, specifically, Bush's decision to wage what in Dean's view was an immoral and poorly conceived war with Iraq. There was truth to the media's assessment: Dean was direct; Kerry did talk like a senator; and, historically, senators, especially those who talked like senators, did not do well in presidential races. From Gary Hart to Paul Simon, from George McGovern to John Glenn, senators as presidential candidates had often failed, usually badly. The last sitting senator to receive his party's nomination and win the White House was John F. Kennedy—in 1960.

As autumn had unfolded, Kerry became increasingly distressed over both his inability to advance his message and, more to the point, his failure to mount any serious challenge to Dean. A week after his announcement tour, he accepted the resignation of his director of communications, Chris Lehane. Then, just this week, after mulling it over for a month, he replaced his campaign manager, Jim Jordan, with Mary Beth Cahill. Much of the media coverage he had gotten since Monday focused on his campaign-staff shake-up. Still, Kerry knew that when the press is talking about the campaign and not the candidate's message, there's a problem. So, as the week passed and the buzz over Jordan's firing escalated, Kerry decided he needed to refocus the attention he was getting. It was time for the press to cover what he was saying, not his personnel. He would force the media to comply, or so he hoped, by giving the speech of his career.

In his hotel suite, Kerry picked at his lunch, a steak ordered from Jesse's Embers, a local steak joint—no Whopper for him today—and worked on the speech. As the afternoon passed, a central theme for the speech emerged. A few months ago, Ralph Cooper, a friend of Kerry's from Massachusetts and one of the original Doghunters, a group of Vietnam veterans who had worked for Kerry in his past Senate races, had called Kerry "the real deal." Kerry had been thinking about the phrase because Cooper, who was living with cancer, had been on his mind a lot lately. It was guys like Ralph Cooper, Kerry believed—veterans who depend on government and military benefits—who were getting a raw deal from Bush, who had reduced federal support to veterans programs. The Bush Administration talked about veterans (although few people close to Bush actually *were* veterans), but it did little to help veterans and their families in terms of federal funding.

Soon, Kerry and his aides came up with a parallel on which to base the speech: the Raw Deal of Bush versus the Real Deal of Kerry. This would be a speech, then, about authenticity—about keeping faith, fulfilling promises, being who you really are. John Kerry was a veteran, and he had the commendations to prove it: a Bronze Star, a Silver Star, and three Purple Hearts. He didn't have to play dress-up and fly onto the deck of an aircraft carrier to feign military credentials.

Kerry knew tonight's speech had to be a winner. He would be studied not only by the audience of Iowa Democrats but also by a press corps who would be looking to see how he and his campaign were faring with a new campaign manager. By the end of his prep session, Kerry felt confident. He put on a navy-blue suit and his lucky Harley Davidson tie, and he was ready to go.

It was going to be hard for Kerry to get any discernable share of the spotlight. The star of the evening, the media had decided, was New York Senator Hillary Rodham Clinton. Although six of the candidates were going to address the dinner, the organizers had invited Clinton to give the keynote address and serve as the master of ceremonies. Party officials said they needed Clinton's star power to sell out the event, but rumors circulated in Democratic circles that Clinton might find a way to enter the race, which added to the gossipy nature of the evening and called into question the real reason the organizers had asked her here. After all, Clinton sometimes behaved like a candidate, and the media covered her as if her candidacy was imminent. Apparently, it was beside the point that Clinton had repeatedly stated she was not going to run for president in 2004 (although some of her denials did sound rather lame) and that, up until now, she had made no effort to assemble anything resembling a presidential campaign. Her mere status as political luminary—former first lady, now a senator—made her presidential material. Tonight, she might even make more veiled hints, more inside jokes, more unconvincing denials.

Before the dinner, Kerry attended a rally downtown in an enclosed shopping area. Surrounded by his family and friends, he spoke briefly to the crowd of 1,000 supporters before being led in a parade of veterans and firefighters—the firefighters' union was the only national labor union to endorse him thus far—through a long network of glass-encircled skywalks that wound its way through the business district of Des Moines to the Veterans Memorial Auditorium. The procession even included the Isiserettes, a drum-and-dance corps that provided a constant beat for the 15-minute walk from the rally to the auditorium. When the parade reached its destination—*The New York Times* called Kerry's entrance to the dinner "a sensation"—Kerry took his place at a dinner table near the stage. Tonight's stage was a large, circular rostrum with no podium, which meant that each speaker would have to address the audience "in the round." At his table, Kerry was joined by his wife, Teresa Heinz Kerry; members of his Iowa campaign staff; and guests representing veterans, firefighters, teachers, and family farmers. The interior of the auditorium was plastered with thousands of signs and posters. On one wall was an enormous sign Kerry could not miss. It read JOHN KERRY PRESIDENT.

At this point in the campaign, Kerry had appeared on several programs with some or all of his opponents, but tonight was different. The entire political establishment of Iowa was either in the room or watching on television, as was a larger, national audience, since the dinner was being telecast live on C-SPAN. As a result, the event was not like any of the others that had taken place in the political season to date. Kerry ate his dinner and waited for the program to begin.

Three candidates were not there—the Reverend Al Sharpton, Senator Joseph Lieberman of Connecticut, and former NATO commander and retired army general Wesley Clark, all of whom had decided to skip the Iowa caucus. Those present were Congressman Richard Gephardt of Missouri, with whom Kerry had served in the Congress for years, although the two had never been particularly close; Senator John Edwards of North Carolina, a good campaigner who had done surprisingly well for someone whose only political experience consisted of his five years as a junior senator; Dr. Howard Dean, whose campaign had spent a fortune on the organization and decorations for the evening; and two candidates who were attracting modest support, Congressman Dennis Kucinich of Ohio and former Senator Carol Mosley Braun of Illinois.

Clinton began the program with her keynote address. Wearing a black pants suit and a white blouse trimmed with antique-lace collar and cuffs, she had a commanding presence onstage. "I know that we're enthusiastic and excited tonight because we have great candidates," she said, confronting the charge made by some pundits that the current field of Democratic candidates was weak. "Those were comments that were made in 1992 when Bill Clinton and Tom Harkin were running," she said, referring to the Iowa senator, who was at the dinner. "Never forget. Never forget pundits and polls don't pick presidents. People pick presidents."

Her keynote address finished, Clinton introduced each speaker. She had asked each campaign to write the introduction she would read for its candidate, so she wouldn't be accused of showing favoritism. Once she had read an introduction, the candidate made his way out of the audience from the table where he was eating dinner onto the stage to give his speech using a handheld microphone. Only Dean broke the pattern. When Clinton introduced him, the spotlight swirled nervously around the auditorium until it located Dean standing in the balcony among a gaggle of his supporters, the die-hard fans who had come to be known as Deaniacs.

It would be weeks still before the Perfect Storm would emerge, when Deaniacs from across the country converged on Iowa to go door to door, each wearing a bright orange toboggan as a sort of badge of honor, to tell Iowans why they had to vote for Dean. Nor were tonight's Deaniacs resorting to the tricks they had used in the past to get media attention. No throng was rattling prescription drug bottles filled with coins and yelling, "The Doctor is in! The Doctor is in!" This happened at many Dean gatherings when he first hit the national scene and it became known that he really was a physician. No one was holding signs with cute sayings like I SEE DEAN PEOPLE (a reference to the line from *The Sixth Sense,* "I see dead people"). Tonight the Deaniacs were rather ordinary-looking and -sounding, as they waved their standard placards—DEAN FOR AMERICA! most said—and cheered on their political hero. Dean waved from the balcony before he made his way down to the main floor of the auditorium and bounded onto the stage to give a version of the speech he had given so many times before, the thrust of which said that it was time for change to come to America.

Another night, Dean's performance would have stolen the show— he was even last to speak—but not tonight. After Clinton had read Kerry's introduction, a short piece heavy on biography written by David Wade, Kerry took the stage and, with focused energy and a clear delivery, began his speech. As he and his aides had worked on it all afternoon, the speech had become more hard-hitting, more overtly challenging, more in-your-face than the stump speech he had been giving since his announcement tour in September. Part of the logic behind the new speech was simple: since Kerry was sinking in the polls, he had nothing to lose by going on the attack. So, tonight's speech was the occasion when he finally used the phrase that the veteran in South Carolina had given him weeks ago. "George Bush thought he could play dress-up on an aircraft carrier," Kerry told the partisan audience, "and stand up in front of a sign that said 'Mission Accomplished.' He thought we wouldn't notice that the troops are dying." Kerry could feel the visceral response of the audience. He felt he was connecting with the crowd in a way he had not connected with audiences in the past.

Kerry continued his assault on Bush. "If George Bush wants to make national security an issue in this campaign," he said, "I have three words for him that I know he'll understand." A short pause for dramatic effect. *"Bring it on!"* Not surprisingly, the crowd, eight thousand strong, erupted into one of the loudest ovations of the night, and one reason for the reaction was the simple fact that it was Kerry—the deliberate politician who had been known on occasion to lapse into Senatespeak—who was now willing to go to the level of red-meat attack. That language—what he said and the way he said it—was certainly not senatorial.

Given that Dean had based much of his campaign on attacking Bush for fighting an illegitimate war in Iraq, and given that Dean himself had no military experience, it was a statement—*Bring it on!*—that Dean could not have used. As it turned out, Edwards had first used the phrase back on February 22, 2003, when he was addressing the Democratic National Committee and hurled a challenge at Bush, saying, "If you want to talk about the insiders you've fought for versus the kids and families I've fought for, here's my message to you: 'Mr. President, *bring it on!*'" Edwards had used the phrase four and a half months before Bush taunted the Iraqi militants with it during his press conference on July 2 in the Roosevelt Room. Kerry had used a version of the phrase in his announcement speech in early September, but on the advice of his media consultant, Robert Shrum, he had decided that the original passage using the phrase was too "bellicose," as *The New York Times* would report, so he altered it. Now, more than willing to get tough, whatever the cost, Kerry used the challenge in as provocative a context as possible.

As he felt the electricity in the room, Kerry was convinced that making Bush his target had been the right decision. Still, before he could run against Bush, he had to win the nomination, and at the moment he was not succeeding at that. Things had gotten so bad that in this very month a poll conducted by the *Boston Herald* would show Kerry trailing Dean in his home state of Massachusetts by nine percentage points, 33 to 24. So, it was time to confront Dean as well— if not directly, then indirectly. "We need to offer answers," Kerry told the crowd that night, "not just anger"—a jab at Dean, who had made his reputation by casting himself as the "angry man." "We need to offer solutions, not just slogans. So, Iowa, don't just send them a message next January, send them a president." As he left the stage and the crowd's roar filled the auditorium, Kerry knew his words had hit home.

Although the story was never reported by the national media, the evening's proceedings revealed dire problems in the Dean campaign. Before the dinner, the campaign had held a rally where Melissa Etheridge was supposed to perform, but when she did not appear, a substantial part of the audience left without staying to hear Dean speak and, more important to the campaign, without proceeding on from the rally to the dinner in a caravan of busses that the campaign had rented. In fact, when the busses pulled up in front of Veterans Memorial Auditorium—and much was made of the fact that forty-eight busses would be needed to transport the Deaniacs to the dinner—a full third of them were empty. If there was ever a metaphor for the Dean campaign, this was it: beyond the hype, beyond the razzle-dazzle, the support for the campaign simply was not as strong as the media had reported. The empty busses might have been one reason why, the next morning at a hotel restaurant in Des Moines, Joe Trippi would be seen in a heated argument with other senior Dean staffers. "Well, if you guys want me to leave, that's fine—I'll just leave," Trippi was heard to say that morning.

For Howard Dean, the problem with the Jefferson Jackson Dinner was not his unreported weak support. His problem was much more basic. John Kerry had decided to get serious about running for president, and his remarks at the Veterans Memorial Auditorium served as a warning to the other campaigns, the media, and the Democratic Party as a whole that he would do whatever it took to get the nomination. As Kerry had told the young reporter from the *Des Moines Register* that morning, he was in this race to win.

Returning to his hotel after the dinner, Kerry was stopped by crowds cheering in the street. Among the mob was a cluster of the Veterans Brigade for Kerry, a group that was helping the campaign put together the statewide grassroots organization it was going to need to win the caucus. Kerry went over to greet his friends, and before he knew it he was on his way with them to the Raccoon River Grille, where he stayed until well past midnight. He was in a good mood; he knew that, with tonight's performance, he had started to turn his campaign around. He had proof, too: following his speech, Iowa's governor Tom Vilsack and his wife, Christie, let him know they were now ready to support him. Other state politicians made similar gestures after the dinner as well.

On so many Iowa nights, Kerry would drive with his staff in his minivan, and off in the distance among the prairie lights he would see the town that was his destination before he reached it. That's the thing about traveling in Iowa. You can often see where you're going before you get there. Despite all the people who had written off the Kerry campaign, Kerry never did. He always knew that, one way or another, his campaign would allow him to connect with voters. Tonight, Kerry turned his campaign around, a campaign that had begun—officially—some weeks back, in South Carolina.

Even by South Carolina standards, it was swelteringly hot for this time of year, early September. For weeks, the senior staff of the Kerry campaign—Jim Jordan, Robert Shrum, Chris Lehane, and others—had debated among themselves about the best location for their man to make the announcement that he was running for president. It was finally decided that the speech would be made in Mount Pleasant, South Carolina, a small town outside of Charleston. As the backdrop for the speech, the campaign would use the USS *Yorktown,* a retired aircraft carrier that had seen duty from 1943 until 1970. Known as "The Fighting Lady," the carrier had seen extensive combat in World War II, the Korean War, and Vietnam. Since her retirement, she had been moored at Patriot's Point on the harbor near Charleston. The choice of the *Yorktown* as backdrop was obvious enough: it was meant to remind the public of Bush's jet ride onto the deck of the *Abraham Lincoln,* where he had declared the main military action in Iraq a "mission accomplished"—a photo-op that seemed less brilliant in retrospect, even to Republican partisans, than it had on the day it was staged. At the same time, the choice of the *Yorktown* was emblematic of one of the fundamental decisions Kerry had made. A decorated navy veteran who had seen two tours of duty in Vietnam, Kerry was going to embrace his military record and make his service a cornerstone of his campaign.

Until now, candidates, especially presidential candidates, had steered away from the subject of Vietnam and its difficult legacy. Early on in his presidential campaign in the summer and fall of 1999, George W. Bush had had to answer allegations that in 1968 he had used his politically connected father, a congressman from Texas at the time, to pull strings to get him into the Texas Air National Guard. Otherwise, young Bush would have been drafted and likely sent to Vietnam. Al Gore had been a journalist in the army in Vietnam and had never seen active combat. Bill Clinton was forced to answer charges in the 1992 race that, because he'd asked a family friend to write a letter on his behalf, which subsequently helped him to avoid the draft, he was a draft dodger.

Kerry's history on Vietnam was not uncomplicated, either. After he had served his tours of duty during 1968 and 1969, he had come home and joined the movement that opposed the war. As a presidential candidate, he was open to charges that his antiwar efforts in the early 1970s were un-American. More than likely, his connections, no matter how tenuous, to Jane Fonda, who was also a controversial figure in the antiwar movement, would be used against him. Still, in his Senate races, Kerry had never shied away from his Vietnam record. So, as he prepared for his presidential campaign, he made up his mind not to start distancing himself from his Vietnam experience now.

Indeed, he did just the opposite; he went out of his way to embrace his memories of Vietnam. On the day he was to make the announcement that he was running for president, Kerry began his day, once he had showered and started to get dressed, by putting on his dog tags, which he would wear under his shirt. He rarely wore his dog tags, only on special occasions. Later in the morning, he met with Skip Barker, a veteran from Alabama who was now a lawyer and a cotton farmer, with whom he reminisced about their mutual friend Don Droz, who had been killed in Vietnam. Still later, Kerry had a late breakfast with the crewmen from the two swift boats he commanded on the Mekong Delta in Vietnam, and when he entered the hotel meeting room where the breakfast was being held, the crewmates stood in unison to salute him—he was still their commanding officer.

For hours on the morning of September 2, the crowd filed in to fill the 800 folding chairs that had been set up on a grass field with a view of the *Yorktown*. A high school marching band arrived accompanied by hordes of students. Hundreds of local residents streamed in, many of them wearing Kerry buttons. A contingent of Vietnam veterans filled a set of bleachers to one side of the stage. Wearing navy-blue polo shirts and a variety of military insignias, they formed a kind of platoon—a testament to the fact that Vietnam veterans now made up a majority of the veterans in America. They had turned out to see one of their own—some had watched him this morning as he made the round of network morning shows—since it was not lost on them that Kerry had chosen to embrace his service in Vietnam rather than shy away from it.

Soon all of the folding chairs were filled and the overflow crowd waited for Kerry to arrive. As they did, the midday sun blazed down, pushing the temperature up to 100 degrees. Umbrellas appeared here and there as women tried to shield themselves from the sun. Everywhere, handheld paper fans flapped back and forth. The audience was wilting before Kerry even got there.

This kind of poor coordination was one of the myriad problems then plaguing the campaign. No doubt it had been a wise move to launch the campaign with Kerry standing before an aircraft carrier in an important Southern state. But it seemed that no one had foreseen that by holding a rally in South Carolina in oppressive noontime heat the message would be sacrificed to the weather! Still, the decision had been made to hold the rally now, rather than at twilight when the image would have been the same and the temperature 20 degrees or more cooler, so it had to take place as planned. Eventually, the time came for Kerry to take the stage.

He was preceded by former senator Max Cleland, whose life story had always been an inspiration to Kerry. Cleland, now 62, was on a mission: he was determined to exact revenge on George W. Bush for his part in helping to defeat him in 2002 when he was running for reelection to the Senate from Georgia. Coming back from Vietnam in 1968 a triple amputee, Cleland had believed his life was over. It took him an hour and a half to get dressed in the morning; how could he possibly have a career? Who would hire a triple amputee? He turned to politics. After Cleland was elected to the Georgia state senate in 1970, President Jimmy Carter appointed him head of the Veterans Administration in 1976. After four terms as Georgia's secretary of state, he was elected to the U.S. Senate in 1996 but was then targeted as vulnerable six years later by the Bush White House. The low point in 2002 came when Cleland's opponent, Saxby Chambliss, a Georgia congressman supported by Bush, ran ads that juxtaposed Cleland's face with those of Saddam Hussein and Osama bin Laden. Cleland was obviously weak on national defense, the argument went, because he had opposed the creation of the Department of Homeland Security. (Actually, he opposed the way Bush was designing the new department.) Following his defeat, Cleland warned Kerry that he would be ruthlessly attacked if he ran for president. Over the coming months, Cleland fell into a deep depression. When Kerry called to ask him to help, he said he would do whatever he could. Perhaps campaigning for Kerry might even help him overcome his depression.

When Cleland was announced, a huge roar rose up from the audience. An assistant pushed his wheelchair up the ramp onto the stage, and he was followed by a stream of veterans, all of whom had served with Kerry in Vietnam. Finally, as the sun pounded down on the crowd and a prerecorded rendition of "Anchors Away" blared over the public-address system, Kerry himself appeared. Accompanied by Teresa Heinz Kerry and other friends and dignitaries, he strode slowly up the ramp to take his place behind Cleland onstage.

In his introduction, Cleland, calling him "my brother," praised Kerry for his military experience. "Thank you, Max Cleland," Kerry said, "for your friendship, your inspiration, and your patriotism." Then Kerry brought up David Alston, an ordained Baptist minister—and a South Carolinian—who had served with Kerry in Vietnam on the Mekong Delta in early 1969, to give the benediction. Finally, Kerry launched into his speech, which took direct aim at Bush—not at Howard Dean or any of the other Democratic candidates he would challenge in the primaries.

"Every time that our country has faced great challenges," Kerry said, "we have come through—and we have come out stronger—because courageous Americans have done what's right for America. This is a time for the same kind of courage." He would use that word—"courage"—so often in the speech that *The New York Times* made a point of printing the total: ten. Why not? The campaign's slogan was "The Courage to Do What's Right for America." "I reject," Kerry continued, "George Bush's radical new vision of a government that comforts the comfortable at the expense of ordinary Americans, that lets corporations do as they please, that turns its back on the very alliances we helped to create and the very principles that have made our nation a model to the world for over two centuries. George Bush's vision does not live up to the America I enlisted in the navy to defend."

Dressed in a dark blue suit—although he took off his jacket because of the heat—Kerry looked the epitome of a candidate. Only later did the power of the moment sink in: this was not the same kind of speech he had made so many times in the past—hundreds of them after his return from Vietnam, when he became a part of the antiwar movement; hundreds more throughout his four successful campaigns for the Senate; or the countless hundreds on the Senate floor. No, this speech was like no other he had given, because he was doing what he had dreamed about since he saw John Kennedy speak on the Boston Common the day before the presidential election in November of 1960: he was announcing that he was running for President of the United States of America. "I am running," he told the crowd on Patriot's Point, "so we can keep America's promise—to reward the hard work of middle-class Americans and pull down the barriers that stand in their way and in the way of those struggling to join them."

In the speech, Kerry brought up Bush's flight to the *Abraham Lincoln*, as well as the Roosevelt Room press conference. "This president has failed to make us as safe as we should be," Kerry said. "Being flown to an aircraft carrier and saying, 'Mission accomplished' does not end a war. The swagger of a president saying, 'Bring 'em on' will never bring peace." The crowd responded, but nothing like future audiences would, when Kerry changed the way he characterized Bush's actions and when he took Bush's taunt and turned it back on him. But this passage in the speech stood at the center of a larger dispute within the campaign: exactly how should Kerry go about running for president? Who was his opponent? Bush? Howard Dean? If the opponent was Bush, when and how hard should he hit him?

None of these questions had clear answers for Kerry, and that lack of clarity was reflected in the quality of the speech. His intent was clearer than the speech: only a veteran who knew something about national security would have what it takes to beat George W. Bush. But the delivery of that message was vague and muddled.

The campaign had not found its tone—often a campaign's theme and content emerge only after its tone is established—and its direction was unsure, even aimless. Too many people were fighting over too many decisions. That's why Kerry had stayed up until 2:30 A.M., working with his staff on rewriting the speech. With his network morning-show appearances only a few hours away, he finally gave up and went to bed, only to toss and turn anxiously until it was time to get up. That's also why Kerry found himself making his announcement speech under a broiling noontime sun in South Carolina before an audience that was often too hot even to respond to what he was saying. No wonder the latest Zogby poll in New Hampshire had Dean ahead of Kerry 38 percentage points to 17—a 21-point spread.

After the speech was over, Kerry worked the rope line and shook hands with as many of the hundreds of people in the audience as he could. Then he returned to the hotel to have a lunch of a sandwich and a soft drink in an air-conditioned conference room. At some point that afternoon, a reporter asked Kerry if he thought the speech might have been too mild and, if so, whether he planned to make any changes in his staff—a rumor that had started to circulate. "I think they've done a spectacular job on a lot of things," Kerry said about his staff. "And I think there are some things we could've done better." An hour later, without clearing it with Kerry, Lehane issued a statement on behalf of the campaign saying "there will be no changes" in Kerry's staff. Denying rumors of a staff shake-up was not what Kerry wanted to be doing on the day he announced that he was running for president.

3

THE NEXT
PRESIDENT
OF THE
UNITED STATES

Months before, on the frigid night of January 10, 2003, in New Hampshire, John Kerry crossed a threshold of sorts—and because of who he was, word of it made the papers. He had come to the home of Peter Burling, an elected state official and a good Democrat, to speak to a gathering of some seventy-five potential voters. As Kerry stood in the living room of Burling's farmhouse, a fire roaring in a fireplace behind him, he talked about the upcoming presidential race and the reason for the informal trips that he'd been making to New Hampshire for several weeks now, and suddenly the roomful of people heard him say, "When I'm President of the United States . . ." He paused. Standing there in his shirtsleeves, surrounded by strangers, he had done what he had been carefully avoiding now for months: he acknowledged he was running for president. He finished the statement: ". . . we're going to have early-childhood education." The second half of the sentence was not exactly earthshaking—what Democrat worth his salt was against early-childhood education?—but the first half was so newsworthy that it was reported in *The Boston Globe* on Monday. The newspaper even noted that the historic nature of the phrase—he was running for president, not considering it, not weighing the possibilities, but actually running—had been verified by two sources, a reporter and a Kerry aide, both of whom "have witnessed nearly every moment of Kerry's fledgling presidential candidacy."

Still, the fact that Kerry was running was hardly a surprise. Following the midterm election, a race that saw the Republicans retain control of the House of Representatives and take back the Senate, Kerry hired as his campaign manager Jim Jordan, a 41-year-old native of North Carolina who in the past had worked for Senator Tim Johnson of South Dakota, Senator Robert Torricelli of New Jersey, and the House Judiciary Committee during the period when it was involved in the impeachment of President Clinton. That Jordan had helped run the Senate committee during the midterm election when the Democrats won only twelve out of thirty-four races did not matter to Kerry. He had known Jordan for years and was sure he would do a good job running his campaign.

After hiring Jordan, Kerry had also assembled the beginnings of an excellent staff. From his Senate office, he brought over David Wade, a devoted Kerry loyalist who had served as Kerry's chief Senate speechwriter and as his director of communications (Wade had never worked for anyone but Kerry); Kelly Benander, Kerry's Senate press secretary; and Peter Maroney, Kerry's top fund-raiser. Kerry also lined up Jim Margolis of Greer, Margolis, Mitchell, Burns & Associates to produce his ads, and Chris Lehane, who had been a communications expert for the Clinton White House and the Gore presidential campaign. For Kerry, Lehane would serve as director of communications. Kerry's brother Cameron, nicknamed Cam, a lawyer who had worked on every race Kerry had run so far, would serve as an adviser to the campaign. Cameron took the title of senior adviser, which meant he did a little bit of everything, from writing speeches and ads to planning strategy with Kerry and the senior staff to overseeing fund-raising. Jordan also brought on Robert Gibbs, who would work in communications.

In January, Kerry selected his state chairman for Iowa, a move meant to send a signal that he did not intend to ignore the state, even though Richard Gephardt, who was also running, had won the caucuses there in 1988. By naming a state chairman a full year before the caucuses, Kerry was making it clear that he expected to compete to win in Iowa. To that end, he chose as his state chairman John Norris, a former chief of staff of Governor Tom Vilsack and a recent candidate for the House of Representatives from Iowa. Kerry had campaigned for Norris in his losing congressional race and had been impressed with his energy and political skills. Because of his connections with the governor and his involvement in other statewide races (he had managed the 1988 presidential campaign of Jesse Jackson in Iowa and the 1992 Senate campaign of Tom Harkin and had served as the state party chairman in 1998), Norris understood Iowa's political landscape. In January, in addition to making moves in Iowa, Kerry had started meeting with Jeanne Shaheen, the former governor of New Hampshire who had lost to John Sununu when she ran for the Senate in the midterm, to see if she would either run his campaign in New Hampshire, serve as a national co-chair, or both.

In February, Kerry would bring on as his media consultant Robert Shrum, a mercurial but brilliant political adviser who had worked on numerous successful Senate races—those of Robert Torricelli, Jon

Corzine, John Edwards, and Kerry himself (in 1996)—and who had served as a press secretary and speechwriter for Ted Kennedy (he had written the now-famous "dream shall never die" speech that Kennedy delivered at the Democratic National Convention in 1980), but who was perhaps best known for being at the center of many of the bitter and contentious fights that came to define the Gore campaign in 2000.

Specifically, in the final weeks of that race, Shrum clashed with Chris Lehane and Mark Fabiani, both Gore communications advisers, over whether Gore should challenge Bush on the issue of competency. Lehane and Fabiani felt Gore should confront Bush on his readiness to be president; Shrum disagreed. The rancor that resulted from the feud was poisonous. In the end, Gore sided with Shrum, who won the argument the same way he had prevailed in previous political campaigns—by doing whatever he had to do to win. He could be so ruthless that *The New York Times*, in describing his methods, would refer to him as someone who "has become known as a polarizing figure who dominates and divides a staff, a relentless player of inside politics who will sometimes steamroll colleagues to win an argument." Shrum was also not above taking his fights public, as he did in 1976 when, after working for Jimmy Carter for only ten days, he quit in a huff and attacked Carter in the press. However, if there was one criticism of Shrum that had merit, it was this: having worked on the national campaigns of Carter in 1976, Gephardt in 1988, Bob Kerrey in 1992, and Gore in 2000, Shrum, despite his success in Senate races and his sometime genius as a political thinker, had never been associated with a candidate who had won the presidency. (Carter didn't count, since he had barely worked for him.)

Kerry had some concern about teaming up Shrum and Lehane, who had fought so bitterly during the Gore campaign. But Kerry believed that any disagreements they might have had were behind them. Overall, then, Kerry was happy with the team he was assembling. He was doing so well that more than one paper described the early stages of his campaign as flawless. This was why, on that evening in January in the farmhouse in New Hampshire, he was ready to make his candidacy public.

Later that night, Kerry left the farmhouse and traveled to nearby Dartmouth College, where he appeared before a group of students. During a question-and-answer session, a student asked him if being a Massachusetts senator—read *liberal*—might burden him in the presidential race. "I come to the floor today not as a Massachusetts man but as an American," Kerry said, quoting the celebrated speech about the Missouri Compromise delivered by Daniel Webster on the floor of the Senate in March of 1850, "and I'm running for the presidency of the United States on the issues of America and as an American."

The next day, Saturday, January 11, Kerry hammered the point home one more time—to a reporter. "I'm running," he said. "I'm now a candidate. I'm going to draw the distinctions and make the case to the American people." It was only a matter of time, then, before Kerry found himself on the campaign trail being introduced time and again with one of the oldest clichés in American politics: *Ladies and gentlemen, the next President of the United States . . .* But that was what he wanted. After all, he had been thinking about running for president now for more than forty years.

He was born John Forbes Kerry on December 11, 1943, not in Boston, but in Denver. His father, Richard, an air force pilot, was stationed in Colorado when he contracted tuberculosis, which required him to be hospitalized for an extended period of time. So

Kerry's mother, Rosemary, gave birth to him there in the Fitzsimmons Military Hospital instead of in Boston, where she was a member of the blue-blooded Brahmin Forbes family. She herself had been born in Paris, and Richard, the son of Austrian immigrants, had grown up in the wealthy Boston neighborhood of Brookline, home of the Kennedys. This meant that Kerry and his siblings—his older sister, Peggy, and his two younger siblings, Diana and Cameron—were raised in a home of privilege and gentility. But as the years passed the family learned that Richard's father, Frederick, may not have been as well off as some had thought. Richard, who had a law degree, left the air force to become a foreign-service officer. The perks of a diplomatic job were good—the Kerrys lived in comfortable homes and entertained well—but the pay was modest.

Following World War II, Richard served in a series of diplomatic positions in Olso, Paris, and Berlin. Years later, Kerry would recall riding his bicycle through the streets of East Berlin as a 12-year-old boy, past the bombed-out remains of Adolf Hitler's headquarters. From age 11, Kerry attended boarding school in Switzerland. "John went to boarding school outside Zug," Peggy Kerry says, "which had lots of German students. He was supposed to be learning German, but I think he learned more Italian than German. There was a sense of adventure to all this. But it was kind of a strange new world too. It was a lonely world, in some ways."

At 13, Kerry returned to America, to the tiny hamlet of Concord, New Hampshire, to enroll in an exclusive all-boys preparatory school, St. Paul's. There, he studied hard, made friends, and engaged in such extracurricular activities as playing bass guitar in a rock-and-roll band called the Electras. In 1961, the band recorded an album on which Kerry, according to the album's liner notes, was the "producer of a pulsating rhythm that lends tremendous force to all the numbers."

During these years, with his hero John Kennedy now President Kennedy, Kerry became interested in politics. He loved Kennedy's charisma, his charm, his sophistication. He noted to friends that he and JFK had the same initials. During a brief courtship with Jacqueline Bouvier's half-sister Janet Auchincloss in the summer of 1962, Kerry got to meet Kennedy and spend time with him one day at the Auchincloss mansion in Newport, Rhode Island. Kerry almost missed his chance to sail with his hero on Narragansett Bay. He had called Auchincloss to say he was running late. She blurted, "What do you mean? The president is waiting to take us out on the boat." Kerry later recalled: "I moved that car up to ninety miles per hour. I walked into this room and greeted Mrs. Auchincloss. Then this man who was there, I couldn't see him at first, came over and introduced himself. All I could think of to say was, 'Hello, Mr. Kennedy!' You know, something original like that."

That same summer, Kerry volunteered to work in Ted Kennedy's Senate campaign. In September of 1962, Kerry entered Yale University, majoring in political science. On the day Kennedy was assassinated in Dallas, Kerry was so devastated that, as he would say, "I remember walking around New Haven all night long with a cousin of mine. That was one of those nights where I said, 'We have to prove this wasn't a waste.' " Also with Kerry that night was Dan Barbiero, his Yale roommate, whom he had known since St. Paul's. "We wandered around," Barbiero says, "and we were just stunned, absolutely stunned. John didn't speak that much, because he was really low. It was a huge blow to everybody, but more for John, because he'd known him and because he had admired him so much. I mean, we teased John about his initials and how he perhaps might, one day, be another JFK."

In his senior year, Kerry was invited into Skull and Bones, Yale's storied secret society. At Yale, he was also a member of the Fence

Club, the Yale Debating Association (he won the Buck-Jackson Oratory Prize for best patriotic speech in his sophomore year and the Ten Eyck Oratory Prize in his junior year), the Yale Political Union (he was president during the 1964–65 academic year), and the Yale Young Democrats (1962–63). His yearbook also listed him as a member of the Yale Young Republicans (1963–64), which was probably a prank. As it turned out, there was one particular young Republican at Yale at the time that Kerry knew all about. "John pointed this guy out to me one day," Barbiero says. "The guy was with a bunch of his buddies and making a lot of noise. I looked over at them, and John said, 'Oh, that's George Bush.' And I said, 'Who's he?' And John said: 'You know, his family runs Texas.' John knew who he was, and he was respectful of him. I wasn't very impressed because Bush was sort of a cut-up—a spoiled rich kid—and that's how he came across."

As the Class Day Orator for 1966, Kerry gave the valedictory address at his graduation in May—a speech in which he harshly criticized the draft and the United States' role in the Vietnam conflict. Kerry knew about the draft firsthand: earlier in the year the draft board had informed him that he would likely be called for duty. "Although I did have some doubts about the war in terms of policy," Kerry later said, "at that time I believed very strongly in the code of service to one's country, so I enlisted in the navy." As Barbiero puts it, "We felt that it was our patriotic duty to serve if we were asked and that if we were going to serve, we'd rather do so as officers than just be enlisted, or drafted."

For four months, Kerry trained at the Officers Candidate School in Newport, Rhode Island. In December of 1966, he was stationed on the USS *Gridley*, which had been deployed to Vietnam to guard the Gulf of Tonkin. This meant, Kerry later said, "we were chasing around with aircraft carriers working with the John McCains who were flying the planes." Like many sailors, Kerry knew who McCain was even though they had never met, since McCain's father, Admiral John S. McCain, Jr., was the head of naval operations in Vietnam. At the end of his first tour, Kerry returned to Long Beach, California. His ship was just arriving in port on the night of June 6, 1968, when Kerry, his attention riveted to a portable radio as he sat in his quarters below deck, listened in horror to the live coverage of the assassination of Robert Kennedy, who was shot down in the kitchen of the Ambassador Hotel in Los Angeles. "It was so incongruous," Kerry would say, "to have come back from a place where we were at war and people were dying to this country where in a hotel a candidate for president could be killed."

In Long Beach, Kerry trained to become the commander of a 50-foot gunboat—what the navy called a "swift" boat—which was designed to be used, among other things, to patrol the narrow waterways of rivers that made up the Mekong Delta. When he returned to Vietnam for a second tour, Kerry, now a lieutenant, found himself the commanding officer first of Patrol Craft Fast 44, then of Patrol Craft Fast 94. The operations, known as Sea Lords, carried out by these swift boats utilized, according to Kerry, "a very aggressive, very risky, take-the-pipe-to-the-enemy strategy." This use of the swift boats was new. Two weeks before Kerry went back to Vietnam, the military changed its policy on the use of the swift boats and decided, Kerry would say, "to send them up the rivers to prove to the Vietcong that they didn't own the waters." On one patrol mission, Kerry rushed ashore from his boat to kill a North Vietnamese who was poised to launch a rocket at his crew. For his actions, he was awarded the Silver Star.

On another patrol, Kerry was the commanding officer of the lead boat of a group of swift boats that got caught in an ambush by the North Vietnamese. When one boat hit a mine, which destroyed it and scattered its crew in the water, Kerry ordered his boat to attempt a rescue. In the heat of the battle, as Kerry's boat sustained heavy gunfire from both banks of the river, a Green Beret who happened to be traveling on Kerry's boat fell into the water. Kerry's boat had gone some distance down the river before Kerry realized what had happened. When he did, to quote from the presidential citation Kerry would receive, he "returned up the river to assist, [where he] directed his gunners to provide suppressing fire, while from an exposed position on the bow, his arm bleeding and in pain, with disregard for his personal safety, he pulled the man aboard." Kerry received a Bronze Star with Combat "V." The "V" stood for valor.

During his second tour of duty, Kerry also received three Purple Hearts and the Navy Unit Commendation, but it was during the four months when he was stationed on the Mekong Delta this time that Kerry began to draw unsettling conclusions about the war; namely, that American military and government leaders did not intend to win it. Even worse, the military brass had no intention of changing their strategy. For inexplicable reasons, the military leadership remained committed to an unwinnable war. In the late spring of 1969, once he had received his third Purple Heart—the rule was: three strikes and you're out—Kerry was sent back to the States, where he was stationed in New York City in the Brooklyn Navy Yard, working as an admiral's aide. After nine months, he was so disillusioned that he asked for and received an early release. With his honorable discharge in hand, Kerry planned to run for Congress from Boston on an antiwar platform, but after campaigning for one month, he dropped out of the race and endorsed the Reverend Robert F. Drinan, a Jesuit who would go on to win a seat in the House of Representatives in November of 1970.

While campaigning for Drinan, Kerry appeared on *The Dick Cavett Show* and caught the attention of the leadership of the Vietnam Veterans Against the War, who recruited him to join their organization. Its stated goal was an end to the military action in Southeast Asia. Kerry was eager to join. "I came back," Kerry would say, "with a knowledge of how wrong the war was, how screwed up it was, and how imperative it was for me to speak out." That speaking out took the form of speeches that he gave across the country. His message was straightforward: it was time for the United States to pull out of Vietnam and bring American troops back home. As he became a celebrity of sorts in the antiwar movement, Kerry made changes in his personal life as well: he married the twin sister of one of his best friends, David Thorne.

Her name was Julia, and when she and Kerry married in May of 1970, the event was the buzz of East Coast social circles. Much was made out of the fact that Julia, underneath a veil of Belgian lace, wore the same ivory-hued paper-taffeta silk dress, encrusted with a pattern of red roses and green leaves, that had originally been made for her ancestor Catherine Peartree-Smith when she married Elias Boudinot, the fourth president of the Continental Congress, in a ceremony attended by George Washington and Alexander Hamilton. *The New York Times* depicted the Thorne-Kerry union this way: "Miss Julia Stimson Thorne, whose ancestors helped to shape the American republic in its early days, and John Forbes Kerry, who wants to help steer it back from what he considers a wayward course, were married . . . at the 200-acre Thorne family estate in Bay Shore, Long Island."

Kerry remained involved in his antiwar activities, fulfilling numerous speaking engagements and working on the executive committee of the Vietnam Veterans Against the War. In April of 1971, he made national headlines when he headed up a group of 1,200 veterans who descended on Washington for five days of protest to demand that President Nixon bring U.S. troops home. The protest, from April 19 to April 23, was called Dewey Canyon III, a takeoff on the names Operation Dewey Canyon II, which was a U.S. invasion of Laos that had taken place in February, and Operation Dewey Canyon I, an earlier border crossing. The veterans built a makeshift tent community on the Mall three blocks away from the Capitol and slept there at night, even though the Nixon Administration had won a Supreme Court ruling barring them from doing so. In the end, Nixon could not bring himself to send in the police to arrest the veterans, which was what he would have had to do to remove them.

Kerry tried to contain the more contentious and provocative elements of the protest. For example, he strongly advised that Jane Fonda not be present. "I think Kerry made a big effort not to have me invited to participate in that," Fonda later said, "because I think he wanted the organization to distance itself from me, that I was too radical or something. . . . I went to North Vietnam in July of 1972, so it was not even 'Hanoi Jane' yet, but I was still considered a lightning rod and radical. He knew that they had to get the attention of Congress, and he didn't want any unnecessary baggage to come with them."

One thing was certain: Kerry and the protesters had gotten the attention of the Nixon White House. As the protest unfolded, Nixon held meetings to decide how to handle not just the protesters but, specifically, the young, good-looking Bostonian who was starting to get national media coverage. In one meeting, Nixon suggested that Kerry was a fraud. "Well, he is sort of a phony, isn't he?" Nixon said. "A racket, sure." Nixon special adviser Charles Colson jumped in: "He came back a hawk and became a dove when he saw the political opportunities." That portrayal was inaccurate. Kerry had been unhappy with the war as soon as he returned but remained in the navy long enough to receive an honorable discharge. Nixon, however, didn't seem to know that—or care. Later, Colson sent Nixon a memo in which he reiterated an apparent decision, reached in the meeting, to "destroy the young demagogue."

For Kerry, the highlight of Dewey Canyon III occurred on April 22 when, wearing his combat fatigues—with his medals, ribbons, and Purple Hearts—and cheered on by a vocal band of veterans, he appeared before the Senate Foreign Relations Committee to offer testimony as to why the war should end. Advised by an old friend, Adam Walinsky, who had been a speechwriter for Robert Kennedy, Kerry had slaved away at the speech until he had achieved on paper the style and rhetorical power he felt the occasion deserved. One memorable turn of phrase would come to synopsize much of the antiwar oratory of the period. "How do you ask a man to be the last man to die in Vietnam?" Kerry said. "How do you ask a man to be the last man to die for a mistake?"

In his testimony, Kerry cited stories from veterans about "the absolute horror of what this country, in a sense, made them do." He was referring to the "Winter Soldiers" Investigation, an antiwar conference held in Detroit in February in which, Kerry told the senators, veterans recounted how "they had personally raped, cut off ears, cut off heads, taped wires from portable telephones to human genitals and turned up the power, cut off limbs, blown up bodies, randomly shot at civilians, razed villages in a fashion reminiscent of Genghis Khan, shot cattle and dogs for fun, poisoned food stocks and generally ravaged the countryside of South Vietnam." About the Nixon Administration, Kerry said: "This administration has done us the ultimate dishonor. They have attempted to disown us and the sacrifices we made for this country." Kerry could not say the same about the Senate committee. His historic speech was so well received that Senator Claiborne Pell of Rhode Island shocked the audience by saying in conclusion, "As the witness [Kerry] knows, I have a very high personal regard for him and hope, before his life ends, he will be a colleague of ours in this body."

The next day, Nixon held another staff meeting to discuss Kerry and the protesters. Nixon asked H. R. Haldeman, his chief of staff, to evaluate Kerry's performance. "He did a superb job," Haldeman said. "A Kennedy-type guy, he looks like a Kennedy, and he talks exactly like a Kennedy."

That same day, starting in the midmorning, Kerry lived through one of the most emotional episodes of his life. As a climax to their five days of protest, a large group of veterans gathered in front of the Capitol to throw their medals onto the steps. Because a fence had been built to keep them out, the veterans could only throw their medals onto an area near a statue of John Marshall, the first chief justice of the Supreme Court. One by one, each veteran stepped forward, made a short speech into a microphone, and then flung a medal or some object of similar significance over the fence toward the Capitol. Many wept as they did. They had come to Washington to "return" to the government their medals—"symbols of shame," as some called them—because they could no longer endorse the war in which they had received their commendations.

"People threw their medals or berets or release papers or dog tags or ribbons over the fence into a pile," Kerry later said, "and I similarly did that. I threw my ribbons back, not my medals. Afterward, not immediately at the same time, I went up and threw back medals a couple of veterans had given me and asked me to throw. A Bronze Star, specifically, and a Purple Heart." Years after the event, Kerry was criticized for pretending to throw back his own medals when they belonged to other veterans. "Complete fabrication," Kerry said. "The bottom line is, I threw back my ribbons with everybody else and never thought twice about it." For Kerry, as it was for many veterans that day, the four-hour ceremony was overwhelming. When it was finished, he sat down on a nearby lawn. With his arms wrapped around his legs, he buried his face in his knees and broke down. "I cried for ten minutes," Kerry would say, "because I'd lost friends whose mothers only had the medals that I gave back."

That weekend, Kerry attended a huge antiwar rally in Washington, sponsored by other groups, that attracted more than 300,000 people. But it was Dewey Canyon III and his appearance before the Senate Foreign Relations Committee that made Kerry famous—and a target of the Nixon Administration. Soon he was the subject of what became an extensive investigation by the FBI, and the White House sent out Vice President Spiro T. Agnew himself to attack him. At a conference of radio executives in Paradise Island in the Bahamas, Agnew claimed that Kerry had not slept on the Mall with his fellow veterans but in the posh Georgetown mansion of a friend of his wife's family (which was not true) and that the speech he had given before the Senate Foreign Relations Committee had been ghostwritten by a speechwriter for Robert Kennedy.

Adam Walinsky, the speechwriter to whom Agnew was referring, denied the charge, telling one reporter, "I can understand how the vice president could fail to comprehend how the Vietnam experience could produce such bitter eloquence from a man of twenty-six. But, the fact is, that's what produced it—not some fancy speechwriter." Around this time, in a profile about him in *The New York Times*, Kerry tried to explain what motivated him. Saying he was "not a radical in any sense of the word, just an angry young man," he talked about the larger political picture in personal terms. "My mother was born in France," he said, "and when we lived there, I used to play in the old German bunkers outside my grandmother's house. From listening to her stories, I got a vivid impression of what it was like to live in an occupied country, and when I went ashore in those villages [in Vietnam], I realized that's exactly what I was in—an occupied country."

In 1971, the Vietnam Veterans Against the War published a book called *The New Soldier*, which listed Kerry as the author and David Thorne and George Butler (a friend of Kerry's from Yale) as the editors. On the book's cover was a picture of a group of marines posing with an upside-down American flag, the universal distress signal. *The New Soldier*, the Dewey Canyon III, countless other media events—all seemed to be going well for Kerry and the VVAW. But by November, Kerry had dissociated himself from the group, claiming that "personality conflicts and differences in political philosophy" had forced him out. Some believed that Kerry had left when he learned that portions of some testimony gathered in the "Winter Soldiers" investigation, which had been sponsored in part by Jane Fonda, had been proven false. The group was also becoming too militant for Kerry. The following summer, Kerry, who had gone on to form a more mainstream organization called Vietnam Veterans of America, watched on television as veterans from the VVAW disrupted the Republican National Convention in Miami Beach with violence—the kind of protest, Kerry felt, that stepped over the line.

That fall, Kerry ran for a seat in the House of Representatives from Boston. With his brother Cameron serving as his campaign manager, Kerry fought hard, but, even with the Kennedys campaigning by his side, he lost. Some believed that Nixon had targeted the race because he did not want an antiwar Vietnam veteran in Congress. "In the race," Peggy Kerry says, "there was a Republican candidate and a third-party candidate. I think a lot of what happened was orchestrated by the Nixon White House. It was the third-party candidate who did all of the trashing of John as a Vietnam veteran. They ran ads of Vietnam veterans flying the flag upside down, as if it was unpatriotic, when it really was a symbol of a nation in distress. Then the third-party candidate bowed out and endorsed the Republican. So there were a lot of dirty tricks."

A year later, in the fall of 1973—the year that his first daughter, Alexandra, was born—Kerry entered the Boston College Law School. After graduating in 1976, he took a position as an assistant district attorney in Middlesex County. His second daughter, Vanessa, was born that year. Then, in 1982, the lure of elective office took over again, and he ran for lieutenant governor on a ticket with Michael Dukakis—and won. In 1984, when a Senate seat became available, Kerry ran for the body that Claiborne Pell had predicted he would one day join, and, after a hard-fought campaign, defeated Ray Shamie with 51 percent of the vote.

In the Senate, Kerry, always the prosecutor, realized he could use Senate committees as a way to launch investigations into potential criminal activity. Early in 1986, not long after he had been sworn in by Vice President George H. W. Bush, Kerry heard through gossip channels that Lieutenant Colonel Oliver North, by illegally selling arms, might be funding the right-wing Contras in an effort to overthrow the left-wing regime in Nicaragua. To investigate the matter, Kerry got permission to set up an ad hoc committee through the Senate Foreign Relations Committee. When he went to Nicaragua on a fact-finding mission, he was criticized by no less a Reagan Administration heavyweight than Secretary of State George Schultz. Conservatives claimed that Kerry was sympathizing with the Communists. Nevertheless, based on Kerry's work, which suggested that the allegations were true, the Foreign Relations Committee launched a formal investigation into the matter. As the inquiry proceeded, odd things happened. When an airplane was shot down in Nicaragua, documents found on board suggested a connection between the Contras and the Central Intelligence Agency. Then, in November of 1986, a newspaper in the Middle East reported that the United States had been secretly selling arms to Iran and using that money to fund the Contras in Nicaragua. The ringleader of the operation was none other than Oliver North—the man who had caught Kerry's attention in the first place.

In early 1987, a special committee was formed to investigate what became known as the Iran-Contra affair. When the Democratic leadership in the Senate was putting together the list of senators who would sit on the committee, Senator George Mitchell of Maine and Senator Daniel Inoue of Hawaii, aware of the media frenzy such a high-profile investigation was sure to generate, pulled rank on Kerry and demanded spots on the committee. Ironically, Kerry would not be able to sit on the committee that had grown out of the investigations conducted by the ad hoc committee that he chaired. Not surprisingly, Kerry was infuriated, so the Democratic leadership appeased him by putting him in charge of a panel on terrorism, narcotics, and international operations. This time, he delved into charges that General Manuel Noriega was using his position as president of Panama to engage in drug-trafficking. When that charge proved true, Kerry followed a paper trail that landed him in the middle of the corruption that would all but completely disparage a financial institution called the Bank of Credit and Commerce International. Kerry was only halfway through his first term in the Senate and he had already used his skills as a prosecutor to uncover both the Iran-Contra affair and the BCCI scandal. It was a spectacular start to a Senate career, although it did signal that, more often than not, Kerry was going to use his position as senator not as a way to create legislation but as a platform from which to launch investigations that would profoundly affect the social and political landscapes in America.

I n 1982, Kerry and Julia had separated—in part because he was so consumed first by his work as an assistant district attorney and then by his run for lieutenant governor. It was not an easy separation. The Kerrys endured a grueling and acrimonious divorce and custody battle that lasted for six years before the marriage finally ended in 1988.

In 1990, Kerry was still recovering from his divorce when he ran for reelection against his Republican challenger, Jim Rappaport. Kerry prevailed, with 57 percent of the vote. In 1991, he was asked to chair a select committee charged to look into claims that prisoners of war (POWs) and men counted as missing in action (MIAs) had been left behind in Southeast Asia when U.S. forces had left Vietnam in the early 1970s. No senator had wanted to chair the committee, since Vietnam, and especially the subject of POWs and MIAs, was viewed as a political quagmire. Kerry welcomed the job and, lining up John McCain as the ranking minority member, launched an investigation in which he and committee members made fourteen trips to Southeast Asia, studied hundreds of thousands of pages of documents, and called a string of witnesses to testify. The committee even questioned Richard Nixon and Henry Kissinger about the possibility that the United States had executed an exit strategy from Vietnam that left American servicemen behind.

"The purpose of the Kerry committee," says Monica Crowley, who served as foreign policy assistant to Nixon in his post-presidency for the last four years of his life, "was to explore whether and to what extent the Nixon Administration willfully left POWs in Vietnam in order to secure the peace agreement. Nixon and his former secretary of state, Henry Kissinger, were outraged. They found repulsive the contention that they would use American soldiers as bargaining chips and then abandon them to reach an end to the war. And they set out to shut down Kerry's political fishing expedition with the truth. Kissinger did this publicly by appearing before the committee. Nixon did it privately by offering written answers to the committee's questions. Both men said the same things: the Paris Peace Accords had clear and binding commitments from the enemy that all prisoners would be accounted for and returned. If the Vietnamese violated those provisions, it was not because Nixon and Kissinger had failed to act but because Congress had stripped them of the resources and will needed to enforce those commitments."

Finally, in 1993, after months of often gut-wrenching testimony, the Kerry committee released a groundbreaking report on the possible existence of POWs and MIAs in Vietnam, Laos, and Cambodia. The conclusion stated that "there is, at this time, no compelling evidence that proves that any American remains alive in captivity in Southeast Asia." Although a small but highly vocal rogue element of Vietnam veterans did not accept the committee's findings (this group bought into the Rambo myth that American GIs were being held in cages in the jungles of Southeast Asia waiting to be rescued), the report proved to be a milestone document. In the end it gave Kerry and McCain the leverage they needed to argue to President Clinton that, to put Vietnam behind the nation once and for all, the United States should normalize relations with its former enemy. Ultimately, Clinton agreed, and on July 11, 1995, when he held a ceremony in the

White House to sign the treaty normalizing diplomatic relations with Vietnam, Kerry and McCain were standing at his side.

"At the time the hearings began," John McCain would one day say, "we had a cover of *Newsweek* showing three men who were purported to be American POWs alive. Fact is, we found out later on, these pictures were manufactured. At the time, there was a widespread belief that we had left many Americans alive—and that they were still alive—in Southeast Asia. Kerry's hearings were vital in getting all of the information out before the American people. The committee unanimously signed a report that said there was no compelling evidence—and I use those words very carefully—'compelling evidence'—that Americans were alive in Southeast Asia. Those words were very carefully crafted by John Kerry. In the end we would not have had the normalization of relations with Vietnam and a free trade agreement had it not been for the work that John Kerry did."

The next year, 1996, saw the Republican Party in Massachusetts mount its first serious attempt to defeat Kerry in the Senate. The governor at the time was William Weld, a Republican who had gotten elected by being progressive and, equally as important, likeable. In 1994, Weld, wealthy and Harvard-educated, had won reelection in a landslide with a staggering 71 percent of the vote. In his second term, he continued to post high approval ratings in opinion polls. So the Republican Party convinced Weld to run for the Senate; he was their best bet to beat Kerry. At the start of the campaign, Kerry and Weld met at Kerry's townhouse on Louisburg Square on Beacon Hill and agreed, first, to limit campaign spending to $5 million each and, second, to hold a series of seven Lincoln-Douglas debates. Initially, Kerry had not wanted to debate Weld, but he realized he would sustain more political damage if he refused than if he agreed. Then again, Kerry could more than hold his own as a debater. He would have to, for from the beginning Kerry was the object of attacks by not only the Republicans but also the Boston media, particularly *The Boston Globe*. One article published in the *Globe* argued that Kerry was not a war hero because much of what he had done in combat had been staged for home movies he was making of his exploits there—images to be used in later years when he fulfilled his expectations to run for political office.

Kerry was seen as aloof and arrogant, an out-of-touch patrician. His critics even took aim at his new wife, for after a long period as a bachelor when he dated several women, including actress Morgan Fairchild and Catherine Oxenberg, Kerry had settled down and in May of 1995 married the woman he had dated for two years, Teresa Heinz. The widow of former Pennsylvania senator John Heinz, who had been killed in an airplane crash in 1991, Teresa had inherited the multi-billion-dollar Heinz food fortune and Heinz philanthropies. Specifically, Kerry's opponents attacked Teresa by questioning her loyalty, since she was from Pittsburgh and a Republican. She was also characterized as too rich to be trusted. At a St. Patrick's Day event put on for reporters, the Kerry campaign used humor to address the concerns about Heinz. "How do you like Massachusetts?" Kerry asked Teresa during the event, setting up her punchline. "I love Massachusetts," Heinz said, deadpan. "How much is it?"

Later that summer, Weld went to the Republican National Convention in San Diego to give a speech in favor of abortion rights, a move that served to play up his status as a progressive member of the Republican Party and further endeared him to Massachusetts voters. If that wasn't bad enough, on another day, to prove he was anything but a stiff and calculating politician—he was no John Kerry!—he ended a press conference by leaping fully clothed into the Charles River. As Kerry absorbed hit after hit in the press, Weld coasted along, cruising to what seemed an inevitable victory.

As the summer passed, Kerry watched his poll numbers sink. One poll released on Labor Day showed him with a mere 33 percent of the vote. As each day passed, Massachusetts voters liked their governor more; they seemed poised to send him to the Senate. Before that happened, Kerry finally realized he had to shake things up—or lose. So he made changes. First, he decided to stay full-time in Massachusetts—no more trips to Washington, not even to vote. Second, he brought in a new media adviser, an ally of the Kennedy family, Robert Shrum, who was known for creating pointed, hard-hitting ads. Third, he determined he would spend whatever it took, regardless of the voluntary spending limits he and Weld had placed on their campaigns, to position himself to win in the final days. Kerry had been in public office for fourteen years. He did not intend to lose without a ferocious fight. He also had an overriding motivating factor: if he lost, he would never be able to run for president.

So, on the campaign trail, Kerry began to repeat the one claim he and Shrum felt could defeat Weld: that a vote for Weld was a vote for, as Kerry took to calling his opponent, "the ideological soulmate of Newt Gingrich." In other words, vote for Weld and you were voting for a Republican Senate and the conservative platform being advanced by Gingrich. New ads made by Shrum associated Weld with pictures of Jesse Helms and Strom Thurmond, two Southern Republican stalwarts whose politics—they opposed affirmative action, gay rights, abortion rights, almost anything progressive—were abhorrent to most Massachusetts voters. In one debate—there ended up being eight instead of seven—Kerry held up a DOLE FOR PRESIDENT button to link Weld to the national Republican Party, a party dominated by right-wingers. That Weld was nothing like these men—he favored women's rights and gay rights; he even listened to the Grateful Dead—was beside the point. Or maybe it wasn't. In the last debate, held a week before the election, Kerry asked Weld point-blank if he would vote for Jesse Helms to be chairman of the Senate Foreign Relations Committee. Weld would not say no. Kerry's case was made.

The most dramatic moment in the debates came when Weld, a proponent of the death penalty, attacked Kerry for opposing it. Weld told Kerry to look into the eyes of the mother of a police officer who had been killed in the line of duty—she was sitting in the audience—and tell her why her son's life was worth less than the life of his murderer. After Weld asked the question, a silence hung in the room. The audience waited to hear Kerry's answer. The question was reminiscent of the one Bernard Shaw asked Michael Dukakis in one of the 1988 presidential debates—would Dukakis favor the death penalty for someone who raped his wife?—and Dukakis gave a disturbingly academic answer to the emotionally charged question. But Kerry was no Dukakis. Shrewdly, he attacked the murderer but defended his position. "I know something about killing," he said, a reference to his combat duty in Vietnam that caused a hush to fall over the crowd. It was an honest, unsettling comment—the sort most politicians never make. "I don't like killing," he went on. "I don't think a state honors life by turning around and sanctioning killing." When Kerry was finished, Weld had no response. It may have been the turning point in the race.

In reaction to the article in *The Boston Globe* questioning Kerry's performance in Vietnam, the campaign had contacted crewmates who served under Kerry on the Mekong Delta in late 1968 and early 1969. Among the men who responded were those in the crew of PCF

94, which consisted of Del Sandusky (who had been the chief petty officer), Mike Medeiros (the communications specialist), Gene Thornson (the mechanic), Tommy Belodeau (the radarman), and David Alston (the gunner). At the request of the campaign, they came to Boston (Belodeau lived there) to hold a press conference with Kerry and attest to his conduct.

Finally, on the weekend before Election Day, Kerry held a huge rally in Springfield attended by Ted Kennedy and President Clinton. In the final days of the campaign, Kerry aired a torrent of ads. A voter could not turn on the television or the radio without seeing or hearing an ad either touting Kerry or attacking Weld. The ad buy was so expensive that once Kerry had spent all of the money he had raised, he had to put in another $1.7 million of his own money—an expenditure that shattered the voluntary spending limits to which he and Weld had agreed. For his part, Kerry argued that Weld had negotiated smaller agency fees, which meant, Kerry claimed, that he and Weld had spent about the same amount of money on the ads themselves.

Whatever the truth, on the night of the election, Kerry watched as the early results came in. In a race in which he had once been trailing badly, it now appeared that he was going to win easily. By the end of the night, Kerry had defeated Weld by an eight-point margin. "As the Grateful Dead used to play and sing," Kerry said at his victory celebration before a cheering crowd packed into the ballroom of a hotel in downtown Boston, "'What a long, strange trip it's been.'" Later that night, after his speech, Kerry returned to his townhouse where he held a private dinner with his Vietnam crewmates. Having avoided what could have been his political death, Kerry was relieved as he reminisced with the men with whom he had served so many years ago.

With the election behind him, Kerry focused on what he was going to do next. When Al Gore made it clear that he would run in 2000, Kerry decided he would not challenge a sitting vice president; only Bill Bradley, the former New Jersey senator, would do that. Instead, Kerry focused on his duties as senator. Over the years, critics claimed he was among the more liberal members of the Senate, but his voting record would not be so easy to categorize. In 1985, Kerry was one of the first Democrats to sign on as a co-sponsor of Gramm Rudman Hollings, a landmark piece of legislation, which required the government to balance the federal budget, that became synonymous with the Reagan years. Later, under Clinton, he voted for the North Atlantic Free Trade Agreement and co-sponsored a bill that put 100,000 new policemen on the street. So, on issues of money and crime, he was hawkish. On social issues, he was more moderate, supporting gay rights and a woman's right to choose. His votes on authorizing military action were complicated. In 1991, he voted against sending troops to the Persian Gulf, but he supported military action in Somalia, Kosovo, and Afghanistan.

After 2000, once Bush was elected and Kerry decided to run against him in 2004, each of Kerry's Senate votes carried added weight. In many cases, Kerry had voted to give Bush a go-ahead on legislation—No Child Left Behind, the Patriot Act, the bill authorizing military action in Iraq—because he wanted Bush to have the chance to advance his agenda. The success of that agenda would rest on whether the ideas behind it were good. That willingness to vote with Bush on some issues set Kerry up for criticism. But so had his penchant for pursuing investigations over legislation. As *The New York Times* later wrote, "The rap on Mr. Kerry's Senate career . . . has been that he is more interested in high-profile investigations, like those into the BCCI and General Manuel Noriega of Panama, than in the grinding details of legislative procedure. He has deferred to Mr. Kennedy on most bills involving health and education and has few major bills to his name; when asked to summarize his legislative accomplishments, he often seems to struggle."

In the final weeks of 2002 and the first weeks of 2003, as the Democratic Party adjusted to Gore's decision not to run, John Kerry was putting together the core of what he hoped would be a staff that could win the nomination. With Gore gone—Kerry would have run whether or not Gore did—his competition looked slim. Richard Gephardt, a party stalwart who would get strong union support, did not excite voters; John Edwards was a rising star but had almost no political experience; and Howard Dean seemed to be ready to run as the political reincarnation of Jimmy Carter—a left-leaning unknown governor from a small state—which many observers did not consider a viable strategy. In short, no candidate stood out as a heavyweight who could seriously challenge Kerry. With relatively weak competition, Kerry was poised to claim the nomination based on little more than his biography and political résumé.

This was not an easy time for Kerry. For much of 2002, he had watched his mother succumb to failing health. Confined to her home in Manchester-by-the-Sea near Boston, she eventually became bedridden. Kerry's younger sister, Diana, moved in to look after her. Kerry's mother had never fully recovered from the emotional devastation of losing her husband of fifty-nine years in 2000. That year, she and her children had stood by helplessly as Richard fought prostate cancer. He died in Massachusetts General Hospital on July 29. Not long after his father's death, Kerry had learned that his was one of three names on Gore's short list for a vice-presidential running mate, a competition ultimately won by Joe Lieberman. But because he had lost the chance to be on a national ticket, Kerry wanted to make sure his mother knew of his plans. So, one day in the autumn of 2002, as her health steadily failed, Kerry went to see her. "Mom," he said, leaning over her as she lay in bed, "I think I'm going to run for president." Kerry's mother looked up at him and smiled. "It's about time," she said. Not long after that, on November 20, 2002, she died.

As Kerry dealt with the death of his mother, he got a visit one day from his friend Max Cleland, who had just lost his Senate seat to Saxby Chambliss. President Bush had gone to Georgia five times to campaign for Chambliss, who had run a coordinated campaign of negative advertising and publicity against Cleland that was comparable to the one used by the Bush campaign to take out John McCain in the South Carolina primary in 2000, a race that many observers believe ranks among the dirtiest in American political history. In South Carolina, McCain, who spent five and a half years as a POW in Vietnam in the Hanoi Hilton, where he was routinely beaten almost to death, had his heroism questioned by veterans sympathetic to Bush. Plants appeared at McCain rallys to walk through the crowd and make suggestive comments like, "You know he had a private-duty nurse over there." Flyers were sent out that said McCain's wife, Cindy, had been a drug addict. Push-calls—biased campaign messages, sometimes automated—were made to white voters that contained the line, "Did you realize John McCain is the father of a black child?" That reference was to the young girl McCain and Cindy had adopted after Cindy made a trip to Mother Teresa's orphanage in Bangladesh and became attached to one of the children there.

In 2002, the attack against Cleland was just as ugly. What disturbed observers most was the ad in which the face of Cleland—a man who had lost one arm and both legs in Vietnam—was run alongside those of Saddam Hussein and Osama bin Laden. Chuck Hagel, the Republican senator from Nebraska and a Vietnam veteran, was so horrified that he threatened the party with an ultimatum: "You either take that ad off," he told a party official, "or I'm going public with an ad *for* Cleland." Chambliss called Hagel seven times in one day to try and convince him to back off. Hagel wouldn't. As he told Cleland in a phone call at the time, "Some things are more important than politics." Hagel's threat worked. The Chambliss campaign reedited the ad and removed the images of Saddam and bin Laden.

Hagel was not the only one who was upset. The week before the midterm election, Kerry went to Georgia to campaign for Cleland and raised $100,000 for his campaign.

Still, the damage had been done, and Cleland lost. On the Tuesday following the election, when the Democrats gathered in the LBJ Room in the Capitol for their first weekly caucus after losing the Senate, Kerry immediately walked over to Cleland. As he reached down to hug Cleland in his wheelchair, Kerry had tears in his eyes.

It was several days later now, and Cleland was sitting in Kerry's office in the Russell Building. The loss he had just lived through was the worst pain he had felt in his political career. It rivaled the emotional angst he had experienced most of his adult life as he tried to deal with the fact that he believed he had caused the accident that led to the loss of his limbs.

On that day in April of 1968, Cleland, an army captain and a communications officer, had taken a helicopter to a hill near Khe Sanh, where he set up a radio relay site for an upcoming battle. He was ready to board the helicopter and return to his home base when he changed his mind and decided to drink a beer with some of his friends who were part of the advance team stationed on the hill. As he got off the helicopter, he spotted a hand grenade on the ground. Assuming it was his, he reached down and picked it up. Just when he did, it exploded, blowing off his limbs. For more than 30 years, Cleland believed it was his own grenade that had maimed him, until the summer of 1999, when a marine who had helped to save his life telephoned to tell him that it had not been Cleland's grenade that exploded but one dropped by another soldier.

Cleland felt a deep sense of relief that he had not been the cause of his own tragedy. Now that relief had been shattered—replaced by the knowledge that his very patriotism had been besmirched in a race in which his opponent was willing to destroy his character, with distortions and untruths, simply to win. For the vicious assault waged against him, Cleland placed the ultimate blame on George W. Bush.

"I got beaten," Cleland told Kerry that day in Kerry's office. "I don't want this pain to happen to you." Cleland knew Kerry was going to run for president; should he win his party's nomination, Kerry would then face the Bush political operation. "Listen, John," Cleland went on, "they are going to unleash this incredible slime machine that will trash you, your character, your family, your record, your record in the Senate, your whole approach to public life. It will be this massive, incredible, corporate-funded slime machine that will just drive you nuts and trash you in every way possible. You will feel like you have been through a sieve."

Kerry listened to Cleland as he reminded him that the "slime machine" had started with Lee Atwater, who managed Bush's father's campaign when he defeated Michael Dukakis in 1988. It was also used in South Carolina to destroy McCain in 2000. "You know, they were even push-polling voters there to ask them if they realized John McCain had a black child."

"I know, Max," Kerry said. "I know."

"I don't want you, my brother, being hurt like McCain and I were. I love you and I care about you."

"I know you do, Max," Kerry said, and paused. "But somebody's got to fight."

Cleland looked at Kerry. Kerry had not said *run*, somebody's got to run. He said *fight*.

"Well, if you do run," Cleland said, "I'm in the foxhole there with you until the last dog dies."

I n December, as he made political plans as well as he could in the aftermath of his mother's death, Kerry went in for his yearly physical. He came home delighted with the doctor's report. He was in superb health, Kerry told his wife. But Teresa, the daughter of a physician who often spent her spare time studying medical journals, began to question Kerry. First, had he been given the C-reactive protein test, an inflammation indicator, as she had told him to? No, Kerry said, he forgot to ask his doctor to run the test. What was his PSA, an indicator for prostate cancer? Kerry told her it was 3.4, which his doctor had said was perfectly acceptable; some men have a PSA of between 10 and 20. The doctor saw no warning sign with a 3.4.

However, Teresa remembered Kerry's PSAs from his last two yearly physicals. Two years ago, his PSA had been 2.2. This meant that the number had increased by 1.2 in two years, more than .5 per year. The number itself might be all right, but an increase of .5 or more per year suggested the possibility of cancer. For Teresa, it was a red flag. To play it safe, she told Kerry to go back to the doctor and have his blood tested for C-reactive protein, which *The New York Times* would describe as "a little-known indicator of potentially cancerous inflammation," and get his PSA double-checked.

"He didn't know anything," Teresa Heinz told a reporter about Kerry and his knowledge of cancer screening. "He knew zero. Zilch." The next day, Kerry visited the doctor on duty in the Capitol, who did a C-reactive protein test, which was fine, and re-checked the rise in his PSA, which was not fine. Kerry got the news from the doctor as he sat in a meeting with consultants in a law office in Washington. Kerry's cell phone rang while he conducted the meeting in a conference room filled with a team of twenty-five people briefing him on civil rights. He answered the phone, responded with simple replies—"Yeah." "Yeah." "Right." "Okay." "I'll call you tomorrow"—then hung up and carried on with the meeting. Afterward, huddled in a nearby hallway with David McKean, his Senate chief of staff, he said, "You know, I've gotta tell you that I just got a reading on my PSA and it's high. I'm going to be checked out for cancer." When did Kerry find out? McKean wanted to know. "That was the doctor who called during the meeting," Kerry said.

When Kerry went back for more tests, a biopsy indicated that he had a malignancy in his prostate gland. On December 23, he met with his doctor, who told him that he was in the initial stages of the disease that had killed his father two years earlier. At present, the cancer was contained within the gland, which meant it could be treated with surgery. Had Kerry waited six months—that is to say, had Teresa not noticed the unusual increase in his PSA and sent him back to the doctor when she did—the cancer would have probably broken through the wall of the gland, which would have required radiation treatment. Now Kerry had the option of treatments—surgery or radiation.

In January, as he made campaign appearances in New Hampshire and Iowa, he debated what type of treatment he would undergo. Finally, he decided to have the prostate gland removed, which would virtually guarantee that the cancer would not spread. He had the surgery in February.

Following surgery of this type, a patient normally takes six to eight weeks to recover, but because he was in the first months of a presidential campaign, Kerry took only two weeks off. It wasn't nearly enough, and for weeks Kerry struggled with a lack of energy that ended up having a profound effect on his performance as a candidate. Kerry, though, was unhappy he had to take off even the two weeks. "I was pissed off," he told a reporter about the cancer episode. "I thought, 'Fuck this, why now?' I thought of it as more of a real drag on what I was trying to do, not, 'God, I'm going to kick the bucket.' " Kerry adds, "I looked at it as a challenge, but not as a showstopper. You're dealt a hand, you play it. So I just determined that I was going to get through it. This was part of the test of whether or not I could be president."

Teresa saw the scare for what it was. "I think I saved my husband's life," she would say. And if she hadn't saved his life, she had surely saved his campaign. "He couldn't have run, because he would have had to do the treatments," she says. "And they are awful." Others agreed with Heinz's assessment. "My mother is always concerned about people's health," Christopher Heinz says. "She's a mother, a real mother in that sense. You know, kind of brooding, and always sort of playing the doctor. That's why people call her 'Dr. T' and 'Mama T'—it's because she treats a lot of people almost as patients sometimes. Did she do that to me growing up? Of course she did. That's why I'm now a hypochondriac." About Kerry, Christopher said, "John showed an incredible degree of toughness. I remember being

at the first fund-raiser he did in L.A., which was two weeks after surgery. That's not enough time to really feel shipshape, and John not
only did that event, he went full-bore."

Around this time, Kerry was confronted with more shocking
news. One day, in his hideaway in the Capitol, an office separate from
his suite in the Russell Building, three reporters from *The Boston
Globe* met with him to tell him that, unbeknownst to him, the newspaper had hired a genealogist to run a Kerry family tree. Kerry had
known that his paternal grandfather, Frederick, had committed sui-
cide, but now the paper had details: in 1921, Frederick had shot
himself in the head in a men's room in the Copley Plaza Hotel, a hotel
where Kerry had held fund-raisers through the years. The *Globe* also
discovered that Frederick had been born Fritz Kohn to Jewish parents in Czechoslovakia. He converted to Catholicism, immigrated to
the United States, coming through Ellis Island, and changed his name
to Kerry. Sixteen years earlier, Kerry had learned that his paternal
grandmother was a Jew who had converted to Catholicism, but now
he was presented with the fact that her husband had followed the
same life path. That day in his hideaway, the *Globe* reporters showed
Kerry the paperwork that the genealogist had uncovered. Kerry was
stunned by the revelations—the heritage of his grandfather, the details of his death. "My father never knew his father," Kerry later told
a journalist. "Why did my grandfather kill himself? Obviously, I
have asked myself what on earth went on in his head."

In the winter and spring of 2003, as Kerry was trying to mount a
presidential campaign in the middle of a health crisis, Howard
Dean was beginning to do what at first few people thought he could:
he was making a name for himself within the party. On February 21,

as he addressed the Democratic National Committee in Washington, he used a turn of phrase—an echo of a line coined by the late Paul Wellstone, the unapologetically liberal senator from Minnesota who had died in an airplane crash in 2002—that would come to symbolize much of what his campaign was about. He said, "I am Howard Dean and I'm here to represent the Democratic wing of the Democratic Party." Dean meant, of course, that on the issues where he was liberal—and there were many—he, like Wellstone, was unapologetic.

This notion was disturbing to many members of the Democratic Party. The label "liberal" was undesirable, since a string of losses at the presidential level had been chalked up to too-liberal candidates: George McGovern in 1972, Jimmy Carter in 1980, Walter Mondale in 1984, and Michael Dukakis in 1988. That's why, in 1992, Bill Clinton ran as a New Democrat—translation: a moderate, not a liberal. In 2004, compared to the other candidates who would probably be serious contenders—Gephardt, Edwards, Lieberman, and Kerry—Dean was more liberal. He was moderate on some fiscal issues, but on social matters he was far to the left, having signed the law in Vermont that legalized civil unions for gay people, and on the issue of the war in Iraq he was unwavering: he was opposed to it. Had he been in Congress when Bush asked for authority to take military action in Iraq, Dean said, he would have voted no. "What I want to know," Dean said at a meeting of the Democratic Party of California on March 15, "is what in the world so many Democrats are doing supporting the president's unilateral intervention in Iraq." No other candidate could have spoken out against the war as Dean did, because they had all voted with Bush—all of them: Gephardt, Edwards, Lieberman, and Kerry. What Dean was doing was simple but practical: he was appealing to the Democratic base, the segment of the party that was proud to be called liberal, all those Wellstone Democrats. If he could attract the attention of the Left, he could begin to get some traction as a candidate.

In April, Dean modified his position in a way that ultimately made what he had to say on the subject of war even more effective. Speaking at the Alliance for American Leadership in Washington on April 9, Dean revealed that, while he was opposed to the "liberation of Baghdad," he was not against the general concept of taking military action. For example, Dean said he would not rule out using force against either Iran or North Korea to curb nuclear proliferation. He opposed the war with Iraq because he did not feel that Saddam posed the kind of threat that diplomacy could not have contained. Simply put, Dean didn't believe that Saddam had weapons of mass destruction. Iran and North Korea were different. They did pose a threat, and to contain that risk, the United States might have to use force. It became clear that Dean was anything but a pacifist. He just thought Bush was wrong, as far as Iraq was concerned, and he was willing to say so. He was not antiwar; he was anti-Bush.

On April 17, 2003, a week after Baghdad fell, Dean continued to malign Bush: he published in *Common Dreams* a piece called "Bush: It's Not Just His Doctrine That's Wrong." Dean wrote: "The next president will need to undo the work of this band of radicals currently controlling our foreign policy—who view the Middle East as a laboratory for their experiments in democracy-building, where no such traditions exist. Their approach will drastically change the view that the world has had of the United States." Vowing to "tear up the Bush Doctrine," Dean said he would "steer us back into the company of the community of nations where we will exercise moral leadership once again."

Throughout March and April, Dean's anti-Bush message started to take hold. This fact did not escape the Kerry campaign. "I remember in the spring," Kerry's Senate chief of staff David McKean says, "when Kerry and David Wade came back from Iowa, and Wade said: 'You know, Dean is starting to get some traction out in Iowa.' And I said: 'You know why?' He said: 'Well, the war. You know, John is not doing a very good job explaining his vote. He's just so long-winded and convoluted.' I said: 'Do you think this is going to be a problem?' Wade said: 'Well, I think it could be. Yeah.'"

Problem indeed. In April, Meetup.com, the Internet service that allowed like-minded people to "meet up" without having to go through a political campaign, was setting up events in cities all across the country—in cafés, bars, coffeehouses—where overflow crowds would show up to discuss the candidacy of Howard Dean. "In Seattle, and in many other cities around the country," one Internet journalist wrote, "Howard Dean has the sort of momentum most candidates can only dream about. And this is before he has even made a public appearance in Washington." Nationwide, 23,000 people had signed up on Meetup.com to "meet up" about Dean, compared to only 1,000 for Kerry, and these people were doing something else: they were sending contributions. Dean raised $730,000 over the Internet in the first quarter alone.

On May 3, Kerry had a dismal performance in a debate in South Carolina. He even got his facts wrong when he charged that, under Dean, Vermont had seen an overall decline in the number of adults covered by health insurance. Joe Lieberman defended his vote to allow Bush to use military action in Iraq, arguing that Saddam did pose a threat to the United States, which only gave Dean the opportunity to state his position once again: he was not opposed to war, he was opposed to "the wrong war at the wrong time." It was in the wake of the debate in South Carolina that Kerry himself began to worry about Dean. "Dean had established himself with the elite within the party," McKean says. "A lot of people still had not really heard of Dean, but some knew that this was a guy who was starting to make waves. He was a serious guy. I remember John saying, right around this time: 'You know, we've got to watch Dean. This can be like a prairie fire.' "

Part of Dean's success grew out of Kerry's failure as a candidate. "We lost three or four weeks when John had prostate cancer," McKean says, "and some of his very mediocre performance during the late spring and early summer can be attributed to the fact that he came back too early." But much of it resulted from Dean's ability to tap into the anger the Democratic base felt toward Bush, whom many believed had not legitimately won the election against Gore. "As an outspoken opponent of the war with Iraq," Ruth Conniff wrote in *The Progressive* in May, "Dean has been drawing cheers and lifting the spirits of Democratic activists who are spoiling for a fight. He chastises his colleagues for voting for the war, and for rolling over on the Bush tax cuts and what he calls the 'Every Child Left Behind' education bill." A month later, on June 23, when he officially announced his candidacy at a huge rally in Burlington, Vermont, Dean was nothing short of a political phenomenon. "It is clear that no one on the Democratic side has received the buzz that Howard Dean has been afforded since the campaign got underway," National Public Radio reported. "He has excited party activists in a way that his more established rivals . . . have not." And this from CBS News on July 1: "Dean began the campaign as a long-shot candidate, but the *Los Angeles Times* reports that most political analysts now regard him as a legitimate contender for the Democratic nomination."

Much of this buzz had to do with money. On June 30, a week after his announcement speech, Dean released figures showing that over the last three months he had raised an impressive $7.6 million—

which seemed to indicate that Dean's message was connecting with the party's rank and file and with those Democrats willing to send cash. A less-than-stellar performance with Tim Russert on *Meet the Press* in June had not discouraged the everyday contributor from sending in money, usually over the Internet, although party heavy-weights worried that Dean, who had no political experience outside Vermont, might not be ready for the national arena. Still, during July, more money flooded in. In August, with his candidacy receiving unprecedented media coverage, Dean attracted massive audiences from coast to coast during his four-day Sleepless Summer Tour. There was an aspect of self-fulfilling prophecy about all of this: media coverage brought big crowds that brought more media coverage. All the while, the money just kept coming in.

Needless to say, by now, Dean was demanding the full attention of the Kerry campaign. Kerry himself was concerned, though not un-duly worried. After all, he had been in difficult races before. "As Mr. Kerry was moving through the White Mountains here today," *The New York Times* observed one day in August, "here" being the all-important state of New Hampshire, home of the nation's first primary, "a reporter asked if he was worried that Dr. Dean had been on the cover of *Time* and *Newsweek* magazines—a platform Mr. Kerry would presumably have liked to have had. 'Campaigns have cycles,' Mr. Kerry responded. 'It's early. It's very early.' The senator, who has spent the better part of two years preparing for this, continued: 'I haven't even announced yet. We have some time to create some energy here.' "

Kerry was upbeat because his internal polling showed that, at least in Iowa, Dean was not doing as well as the media said he was. Kerry's polling indicated a three-way race between himself, Dean, and Gephardt, with all three candidates tracking in the low twenties. In

Iowa, then, it was anybody's race. Not so in New Hampshire, where public polls suggested that the Dean surge had happened at the expense of Kerry, who was falling farther behind every day. So, when he could, Kerry took the fight to New Hampshire. On August 28, during an appearance at the University of New Hampshire, Kerry lashed out at Dean and Gephardt, who favored repealing all of Bush's tax cuts, and advanced his own tax proposal. Some Democrats, he said, "are so angry at George Bush and his unfair tax cuts" that they'd repeal them all. Kerry disagreed. He would not raise taxes on "the hardworking middle-class Americans who have borne the brunt of the Bush bust," but would repeal the tax cuts for individuals earning $200,000 a year or more. The people who saw major tax relief, he said, were the top one percent of the workforce—no one else. Otherwise, Kerry said, Bush's economic policies had been so disastrous that Bush, the first president to oversee a net job loss since Herbert Hoover, should be known as the "jobless president."

4

THE TURNAROUND

By September, Dean was the clear frontrunner, or so the media said. He may have come out of nowhere to demand the attention of the party, but some still felt that he wasn't ready for national politics. He started to make some mistakes, as he did on September 3, when he finished a question-and-answer session in a coffeehouse in Santa Fe, New Mexico, by committing what turned out to be a drastic political blunder. Someone asked him how he would make peace in the Middle East. To this, Dean said that, as far as the United States was concerned, "it's not our place to take sides" in the Israeli-Palestinian conflict. There were also, he said, "enormous numbers of the settlements that are going to have to come out." In the ensuing days, Joe Lieberman, Gore's running mate in 2000 and the first Jewish American to be on a national ticket, contended that Dean's statements represented a "reversal of American foreign policy for fifty years"—policy that had treated Israel as a special ally regardless of which party happened to be in power in the White

House. This was one in a series of miscues that Dean made in the autumn, suggesting, as some had said, that a career in government in Vermont had not adequately prepared him for the scrutiny he was bound to get on the national, let alone international, political stage.

But Kerry was unable to take advantage of Dean's gaffes, because his own campaign was in disarray. Leading up to the announcement tour in September, the campaign had divided into two camps that fought about almost everything. The warring factions were Jim Jordan, the campaign manager, and Chris Lehane, the communications director—both based in Washington—squaring off against Bob Shrum and Kerry's family and friends in Boston, among them his brother Cameron and his friend David Thorne. It was, in essence, Boston versus Washington. Cameron and Thorne constantly confronted Jordan, demanding to know why he was not using the Internet to better effect (as Dean was) and why the campaign lacked focus. Another line of conflict that erupted into violent disputes concerned the way Kerry should be dealing with Dean. Jordan and Lehane felt that Kerry should be aggressive in his attacks on Dean ("not in a harsh way, but to point out the differences," Jordan later said). They argued that if Kerry had "the courage to do what's right," he needed to have the courage to stand up to Dean. After all, Kerry had to beat Dean before he could run against Bush. Shrum disagreed, contending that Kerry would look bad if he started to savage Dean.

There had even been a fight over the announcement speech. At Kerry's request, Shrum had written the speech himself, but because the campaign lacked any real focus, the speech ended up being a laundry list of what Kerry would do as president—what he would have the *courage* to do. The speech did not take direct aim at Bush, nor did it even mention Dean by name. This was in keeping with the approach that Kerry had used in dealing with Dean until now; almost always, Kerry was guarded, maybe even to a fault. Jordan and Lehane wanted to make the speech more hard-hitting; they asserted once again that Kerry had to have the courage to fight for the nomination, not just to criticize Bush.

But Shrum would have none of it. He refused to rework the speech. So Lehane had Andrei Cherny, Kerry's speechwriter, produce a second, harsher speech called "The New Patriotism." It was much angrier, a reflection of Cherny's determination to co-opt Dean's "angry man" persona. The first line summed up the speech: "Spring training is over." Throughout, the speech maintained a tone that Kerry was not comfortable with; in fact, Kerry hated the speech. To play it safe, Shrum set up a private meeting with Kerry at the townhouse in Boston to make sure Kerry was going to use his speech, not Cherny's. Shrum felt that Kerry needed to sound moderate and thoughtful. He didn't even like the idea of Kerry going to South Carolina to make the announcement speech there; he surely didn't want Kerry to give Cherny's speech in South Carolina. Kerry agreed with Shrum, much to the dismay of Jordan and Lehane. On the announcement tour, Lehane was distant from the campaign, even going so far as to be critical of Kerry to reporters. The behind-the-scenes campaign feud hit the front page of the papers. What was not known was just how badly the campaign suffered because of its warring factions.

As it happened, the reaction to the announcement speech was so bad—and not just because the audience, the guests, and the candidate had been baked by the sun—that Kerry realized he could not deliver the same speech on the second stop of the tour in Des Moines. So, on the flight from South Carolina to Iowa, Lehane, Shrum, and others frantically reworked the speech, trying to make it more punchy, more spirited. The new version may have been better, but in Des Moines the event was marred by a local politician who screamed—sometimes at the top of her lungs—much of her introduction of Kerry. Most of the yelling grew out of her unhappiness with Bush, no doubt her own attempt to emulate Dean's "angry man" persona. How could the advance team have made such an error? Of all the politicians in Iowa, couldn't one be found who could deliver an appropriate introduction for a presidential candidate?

More mistakes occurred the next day when Kerry, having flown back East to New Hampshire, went to an event staged in Derry at a popular lunchtime restaurant, Mary Anne's Diner, where he listened to local citizens discuss the trouble they were having because of the bad economy. With Kerry positioned at the center of a table, people sat on either side of him. They all had been miked so their comments could be picked up by the large traveling press corps that had been cordoned off behind a rope—the sort that doormen use outside trendy nightclubs—on the other side of the room. The local residents at the table had apparently been instructed not to look at the wall of television cameras filming their every move, but to focus on Kerry. They did so with studied calculation, as if they were auditioning for a reality show on television.

One of the locals was Barbara Woodman of Concord, who told Kerry the details of how she had been laid off by a publishing company. The thrust of her story was inspiring: no matter what she had to do, she was going to make sure her children got a good education. "I don't care how many jobs I have to work," she told Kerry, "those kids are going to college. And if I can, I'll do whatever it takes to make this country stronger." Kerry seemed genuinely touched. "That's moving," he said, dabbing a tear from one eye. Woodman's story was emotional—more than one local newspaper put the picture of Kerry wiping away the tear on the front page—but the event had been so obviously staged, complete with people who looked like movie extras sitting in booths in the diner to make it appear as if the place was open for business when in fact the Kerry campaign had rented it out for the day, that one CBS producer was heard to shout at a low-level Kerry staffer, "This is the phoniest thing I've ever seen!"

The last event on the four-state announcement tour, a spectacular rally outside Fanueil Hall in downtown Boston, was an unqualified success. Thousands of people jammed into the open-air mall to hear Ted Kennedy give Kerry a rousing introduction: "Jahhhhhhhh-hhhhhhhhhn KERRY!"—Kennedy had been using this delivery of late as a way to rev up a crowd before Kerry appeared—*"The next President of the United States!"* With Kennedy as cheerleader, Kerry attacked Bush in a way he had not only thirty-six hours earlier in South Carolina. "Every day of this campaign," Kerry promised the crowd in a speech that was carried live by all of the national cable-news networks, "I will challenge George Bush for taking our country in the wrong direction. . . . We should not be opening firehouses in Baghdad and shuttering them in New York. . . . The United States of America should never go to war because we want to. We should only go to war if we have to."

With his announcement tour now over, Kerry resumed his regular campaign. On the evening of September 4, he attended a debate in Albuquerque, New Mexico, where Dean finally began to draw criticism from his fellow candidates. Tonight, the antagonist was Dennis Kucinich, who hit Dean with the line, "You can talk about balancing the budget in Vermont, but Vermont doesn't have a military."

The following Sunday, Kerry watched on television as Bush addressed the nation from the White House and said that Iraq was the "central front" in the war on terror, before asking for $87 billion to finance the military action taking place there—a figure much higher than the one many in Washington, including Kerry, had expected Bush to announce. Not surprisingly, at the Democratic debate on Tuesday, Bush's astronomical price tag was a topic of discussion. "We cannot authorize or appropriate," Kerry said, "eighty-seven billion dollars without pulling back some of the unfair Bush tax cuts for the wealthiest Americans and investing in the United States of America." At the debate, Dean was put on the defensive when Lieberman questioned the comments he had made on Israel a week earlier. Dean felt so vulnerable that he went on CNN on Wednesday to say that the United States should be "evenhanded" on the Israeli-Palestinian issue but added that he had "since learned" that he "could have used a different euphemism" in talking about the Israeli-Palestinian problem. Dean hadn't made things better and he may have made them worse by using the word "euphemism" to reduce a blunt grasp of a complicated issue to a poor choice of phrasing.

On the Saturday after the announcement tour, September 8, John Kerry was sitting in the living room of his Boston townhouse being interviewed by Douglas Brinkley. For more than a year, Kerry had been cooperating with Brinkley, who was writing a book called *Tour of Duty*, a chronicle of Kerry's experiences in Vietnam and his efforts to oppose the war when he came back. A protégé of Stephen E. Ambrose, Brinkley was a respected historian and the author of significant works of nonfiction on figures like Henry Ford, Jimmy Carter, and Rosa Parks. After meeting Brinkley in 2002, Kerry had agreed to cooperate on the book to make it as complete and accurate as possible. Today's would be one of the last interviews, since the book was scheduled to be published in January and Brinkley needed to deliver the manuscript. Joining them on that day was Kerry's Senate chief of staff David McKean. The three men planned to go to a Bruce Springsteen concert that evening at Fenway Park, after Kerry and Brinkley had finished their work.

Sitting for interviews about Vietnam had never been easy for Kerry. Over the years, because of what he had seen and lived through himself, he had been reluctant to talk about the war, especially specific combat missions that took place during his second tour. But Brinkley, a gentle and sympathetic interviewer, made him feel so comfortable that Kerry went on for much longer than the allotted interview time. After a while, Kerry needed to refer to the diaries he had kept in Vietnam, so the men moved to Kerry's study on the house's top floor to finish the interview. Soon they were interrupted by a phone call. McKean answered the phone. It was Chris Lehane. He needed to talk to Kerry.

Kerry heard Lehane say that he had made the decision to quit the campaign.

"Are you sure you want to do this?" Kerry asked.

Lehane said he was certain.

"Can you tell me why you're quitting?" Kerry said.

"This is just not working out," Lehane said. "Anyway, I need to move on to other things." There were other opportunities, he said, that he needed to pursue.

"Well, it's up to you," Kerry said. "Your decision is final?"

Lehane said that, yes, his decision was final.

When Kerry hung up, he and McKean discussed what Lehane's departure would mean to the campaign. Then, fifteen minutes later, Kerry resumed his interview with Brinkley, but Kerry was clearly distracted. As he answered Brinkley's questions, he picked up his guitar and began to play. When Kerry had something on his mind, he always found that playing the guitar helped him to relax.

Kerry spent much of the rest of the afternoon dealing with the fallout of the Lehane departure. He repeatedly interrupted his conversation with Brinkley to take phone calls. In order to finish his interview with Brinkley, Kerry offered to talk well into the evening, so they cancelled the trip to the Springsteen concert.

At one point, Kerry talked about his favorite Springsteen song, "No Surrender," which he liked because it was about Vietnam. When they had finished discussing the war, the subject of the conversation turned to General Wesley Clark, the former NATO commander during the Clinton Administration who was rumored to be getting into the presidential race. A rumor circulating that day, in fact, had Lehane going to work for Clark once he declared. But Kerry was not worried about Clark. "He won't really be much of a challenge," Kerry said, "but there will be a place for Wesley Clark in a Kerry Administration, if he wants it." For a candidate who was as far behind in the polls as Kerry was, it seemed an odd comment to make.

The next morning, Brinkley appeared on CNN to discuss the rumors that Clark was getting ready to declare. Brinkley said he believed Clark would be a formidable candidate. The race in Iowa, he said, looked like it was now going to be between three men: Dean, Kerry, and Clark. When Brinkley met Kerry for breakfast later that morning, Kerry commended Brinkley on his CNN appearance, but said he was wrong about Clark. "It's going to be a three-way race in Iowa all right," Kerry said, "but the race will be between me, Dean, and Edwards. Not Clark."

A t this point, Kerry should have been capitalizing on the mistakes Howard Dean was making, but he had to contend with internal problems in his own campaign. After the announcement tour, Kerry, his family and friends, and his closest advisers knew the campaign was suffering from these conflicts, and, if they weren't cleared up, they would prove disastrous. The main friction was between Jordan and Shrum, but Lehane had been a part of it, too. The fact that the campaign had not even been able to agree on the speech Kerry had used to announce his candidacy epitomized the problem. If Kerry did not make changes, his campaign was doomed. Now Lehane had forced the issue by resigning. But Kerry knew that Lehane's departure was not the only change that needed to be made.

On September 16, published reports indicated that Wesley Clark would enter the presidential race, having been encouraged, it was said, by Bill and Hillary Clinton, who were privately unhappy that Dean, the most liberal of the candidates, was the frontrunner. John Weaver, McCain's chief political consultant in 2000, had turned down an offer to run Clark's campaign, but Mark Fabiani, Lehane's business partner, was working for him already, and it now appeared that Lehane would join the campaign as expected. To complicate matters, Clark had met with Dean in California, sparking speculation that Clark might actually be getting into the race to position himself as Dean's running mate. After all, Dean, who had no military experience, would need a running mate who did.

On September 16, Kerry was endorsed by one of the most prominent members of the Senate, Dianne Feinstein of California. Any sustained bump Kerry might have gotten from her endorsement was overshadowed the next day when Clark declared at a rally in his hometown of Little Rock, Arkansas, that he was running for president. At first, national polls showed that Clark had a good chance of catching on as a candidate. Then he began to talk. On the day after he announced, he was asked by reporters if he would have voted for the resolution authorizing Bush to take military action in Iraq, had he been in Congress at the time. "I probably would have voted for" the resolution, Clark said. The very next day, he "clarified" his position by saying, "I never would have voted for war." His campaign never recovered from the flip-flop, or from the fact that, as was soon revealed, Clark was not a registered Democrat (he was an Independent) and through most of his adult life he had voted Republican. He was immediately criticized for running as a Democrat only because the party was available to him, not because he was a Democrat.

On September 19, following an interview with WCBS-TV in New York, Kerry had left his microphone on while saying that, because of all the gaffes Dean was making—his comments on Israel, for example—his "bubble's bursting a bit." On September 22, in Detroit, Kerry made headlines speaking at the Detroit Economic Club, where he said about Dean: "Anger and attacks are all well and good, but when it comes to our jobs, we need a president who can build a barn, and not just kick it down." Following the political adage that says one should attack one's opponent in his strongest suit, Kerry decided to strike at Dean's "angry man" persona, which had gotten him to where he was.

The next day, Kerry picked up a vital endorsement in New Hampshire when Jeanne Shaheen, the state's former governor, held a press conference to announce she would serve as the national chair of Kerry's campaign. (In 1976, Shaheen had supported Jimmy Carter before his victories in Iowa and New Hampshire made him the frontrunner; in 1984, she worked as the campaign manager for Gary Hart, who went on to upset Walter Mondale and John Glenn; in 2000, when exit polls in New Hampshire suggested that Bill Bradley might defeat Al Gore, she organized a late-afternoon get-out-the-vote effort that gave Gore a razor-thin victory.) If Kerry was going to stand a chance at winning New Hampshire, he needed the political machine that Shaheen and her husband, Billy, had put together during her years in office, so it was hard to overestimate the value of her willingness to join his campaign, especially at a time when many in the party, not to mention the national media, had come to believe that the nomination was now Dean's to lose.

On September 24, when Donald Rumsfeld said that the United States was "on track" with its reconstruction in Iraq, Kerry waited until the next day and demanded that Rumsfeld resign. "He rushed to this war," Kerry said in comments picked up by the Associated Press. "He has not listened to the military personnel. He and Mr. Wolfowitz proceeded with false assumptions. In their arrogance they didn't listen to General Shinseki. They kicked him out of the way. They stomped on his reputation. And he was right. It did take more troops. These people have proceeded in an arrogant, inappropriate way that has frankly put America in jeopardy."

On September 26, Kerry received his biggest endorsement yet when the International Association of Fire Fighters voted to support him. Speaking for his 260,000 members, Harold Schaitberger, the union's president, said that "just as firefighters have been hailed as heroes for their courage and their sacrifice, so has John Kerry been decorated as a war hero and recognized by his peers and his nation for his guts and his bravery."

By the end of September, Dean had raised $12.5 million since July 1. The total amount he had brought in during the year was $23 million. Kerry's third-quarter tally was substantially less—he had raised only about $4.5 million, which made his total for the year $21 million. As Dean had surged, Kerry had fallen into a slump from which he did not appear likely to emerge. Even with key endorsements, he could not raise money. Clark, meanwhile, raised $250,000 within days of announcing, and Dean was bringing in so much cash that he was probably going to turn down federal matching funds. If he did, he would have no limits on the amount of money he could raise and spend during the primary season and, should he win the nomination, during the period before the general election began. Bush had turned down matching funds in the primary season in 2000, although he had accepted federal funds in the general election, but no Democrat had ever rejected matching funds since the government created the program in 1976 as a response to the Watergate scandal.

If Dean did reject matching funds, Kerry would have to do the same, which would pose a problem for Kerry since his fund-raising efforts were faltering. Kerry might even have to put his own money into the campaign, as he did in 1996 in the final weeks of his Senate reelection bid against William Weld. Because Teresa Heinz was not allowed to use any of her vast wealth to fund his campaign—she could give Kerry no more than $2,000, the current cap under federal campaign financing laws—Kerry would have to rely on his own money. But Kerry did not have a lot of cash. When he married Heinz in 1995, according to some sources, Kerry had as little as $100,000. Even now, because he had signed a prenuptial agreement with Heinz, Kerry had no interest in the vast majority of her holdings. As a result, Kerry's main asset was the brownstone on Beacon Hill that he owned with Heinz. Should his campaign need an infusion of cash, he could always mortgage the brownstone, which was estimated to be worth some $12 million.

Kerry's campaign was still plagued by mismanagement. On September 30, the campaign should have gotten good coverage when Gary Hart, the former senator from Colorado and a presidential candidate in the 1980s, endorsed Kerry. On a conference call with reporters, Hart, who had been thanked by Kerry, tried to explain why Kerry was his pick. "It takes years of preparation, and we just don't hold our candidates to that standard," Hart said, referring to his belief that Kerry was the most experienced candidate on foreign policy. Soon Kerry begged off the line but left Hart on, and the first question posed to Hart was loaded. "How important are endorsements?" a reporter asked. Hart didn't miss a beat. "Not very," he said. When a Kerry staffer tried to end the call, Hart wouldn't be stopped. "I don't think," he said, "endorsements, per se, ever got anyone a nomination." Finally, the conference call ended, but the damage had been done. Not only had Hart undercut the importance of what he himself was doing in endorsing Kerry, his remark implicitly belittled the other endorsements that Kerry had received over the last week. Since Kerry was falling in the polls and his fund-raising was dying off, his only good news had been these endorsements, and now Hart had dismissed them as irrelevant. Nothing seemed to be going right for the Kerry campaign.

In late September, as the résumés of the candidates became a central point of discussion, especially for Kerry, who had based much of the reason that people should vote for him on his biography, a Kerry staffer sent out an e-mail that stated, "You do know that he"—meaning Howard Dean—"is the Dean of Dean Witter, don't you?" *The New York Times* noted that Dean was *not* the Dean of Dean Witter. Maybe he wasn't, but he was sure raising money as though he was. When the third quarter ended, Dean had collected a remarkable $15 million. On the Internet alone, he brought in seven million to Kerry's one. Dean had arrived, effortlessly it seemed, at the center stage of American politics, secured his spot as the frontrunner, and then watched as a history-making deluge of cash came pouring into his campaign.

Deep down, Kerry believed he could still do it. But there was no doubt about it: this nomination was going to be much harder to win than he had ever imagined it would be.

One day in early October, John Kerry, who had to be in Washington to cast votes that his staff felt were too important to miss, walked across the floor of the Senate to see Ted Kennedy. Kerry told him that ever since his announcement tour he had become increasingly frustrated over the direction in which his campaign was going—so much so that he had at times become angry to the point of distraction. Kennedy told Kerry that, based on his observations, he believed Kerry was uncomfortable with his staff. At least, that appeared to be the main problem. Because of this, Kennedy said, Kerry needed to change campaign managers. The shake-up with Lehane had helped, but it wasn't enough. Kerry told Kennedy that he had been thinking about doing just that, and he would take his counsel seriously. Finally, Kennedy had another piece of advice: Kerry should break down the distance between himself and the audience. Get out from behind the podium, plunge into the audience, talk to the voters. Think Phil Donahue, Kennedy said. That would help Kerry loosen up—be himself more, be free to crack jokes, be funny.

Later that week, on Friday, October 3, the candidates appeared at a meeting of the Democratic National Committee in Washington. Clark got the most media coverage because he was new to the race— he had already surged to the top of many national opinion polls—

and because so much attention was focused on whether he was really a Democrat. "Before I say another word," Clark said, "I want to make one thing clear. I'm pro-choice. I'm pro–affirmative action. I'm pro-environment, pro-education, pro–health care and pro-labor. And if that ain't a Democrat, then I must be at the wrong meeting." Kerry, who spoke last, could not resist offering a dig. "I am proud that I stood against Richard Nixon, not with him," Kerry said, referring to the fact that Clark had voted for Nixon. "I know what it's like to be spied on by the government, because that's what they did to me when I came back and stood up against the war."

Next, Kerry attacked Dean, then Bush. Only a month ago, Kerry had been unwilling to attack either of them. But as the month had passed and pressure on him grew, Kerry decided to take the advice that, ironically, had been put forth by Lehane, and was still being advanced by Jordan: to attack both Bush and Dean. His willingness to go on the offensive was the basis of what ended up being his campaign's turnaround. So, today, before the DNC, Kerry said three different times that *he* stood for "the Democratic wing of the Democratic Party"—a blatant attempt to co-opt the line that Dean had co-opted from Paul Wellstone. Finally, Kerry took aim at national security, the issue on which Bush was going to build the very foundation of his campaign. "We need to go right at him," Kerry told his fellow Democrats. "Remember, they can't find Osama bin Laden. They can't find Saddam Hussein. They can't even find a leaker at the White House"—a reference to whoever had illegally leaked to a reporter information about Joseph Wilson, a career American diplomat, and his wife, who worked for the CIA.

But the month of October was dominated by one topic: the vote on Bush's request for $87 billion to finance the United States' military action in Iraq. Actually, the expenditure included $66 billion to pay for the military action in Iraq *and* Afghanistan, as well as a little over $18 billion for, to quote the Associated Press, "retooling Iraq's oil industry, its court system, and the rest of its economy and government." On Friday, October 17, the appropriations bill was voted on in the House and the Senate. The vote was not dramatic; the outcome was never in doubt. The bill passed in the House by a total of 303 to 125 and in the Senate by 87 to 12. Two of the "no" votes in the Senate came from John Kerry and John Edwards. "The best way to support our troops and take the target off their backs," Kerry said about his vote, "is with a real strategy to win the peace in Iraq—not by throwing eighty-seven billion dollars at George Bush's failed policies. I am voting 'no' on the Iraq resolution to hold the president accountable and force him finally to develop a real plan that secures the safety of our troops and stabilizes Iraq."

A little more than a week later, on October 26, at a ninety-minute debate in Detroit sponsored by the Fox News Channel and the Congressional Black Caucus Institute, the discussion about Iraq shifted from whether or not the United States should have gone to war in the first place to the vote on the appropriations bill. Tonight, Lieberman, who voted for the funding, attacked Kerry and Edwards for voting against it. "I don't know how John Kerry and John Edwards can say they supported the war," Lieberman said, "but then opposed the funding for the troops who went to fight the war that the resolution that they supported authorized." Kerry shot back: "Well, Joe, I had seared in me an experience which you don't have, and that's the experience of being one of those troops on the front lines when the policy has gone wrong. . . . Our troops are today more exposed, are in greater danger, because this president didn't put together a real coalition, because this president's been unwilling to share the burden and the task." For his part, Clark waffled just as much on whether he would have voted for the funding as he had on whether he would have voted for the war. "I've been over Wes Clark's record and statements on this so many times," Lieberman said. "I heard him tonight. He took six different positions on whether going to war was the right idea."

It was not the last time the issue of the war in Iraq would be debated in the campaign. The appropriations vote had simply brought the issue to the forefront. This most likely ended up helping Dean, who had been vocal in his opposition to Bush's war long before the other mainstream candidates were. In fact, with their votes against the appropriations bill, it now appeared as if Kerry and Edwards were coming around to the position that Dean had held for months, regardless of whether that was an accurate representation of their views on the war.

I n Iowa on Halloween, Kerry was ready to advance a new line of attack on Dean. Dressed in blue jeans, two flannel shirts, a bright orange safety vest, and LL Bean duck boots, Kerry met with a small bunch of supporters in a machinery shed of a farm owned by Ryan McKinney near Colo, Iowa. Talking to his supporters, as well as a pack of local and national reporters, Kerry criticized Dean for opposing a 1994 ban on assault weapons, which, Kerry noted, had gotten Dean the blessing of the National Rifle Association when he was governor of Vermont. Kerry said he had supported the assault-weapons ban throughout the 1990s. (In 1992, Dean had gone so far as to sign an NRA questionnaire and to say he would "oppose restrictions on [the ownership of] semi-automatic firearms.") Standing in the machinery shed, Kerry said, "I've fought the NRA from Day One and I've been on their list since Day One."

Then, picking up a 12-gauge shotgun and accompanied by Buck,

McKinney's English pointer, Kerry headed out of the shed and entered a nearby cornfield. Within five minutes, Buck spotted a pheasant. As the dog dashed for it, the bird flew up into the air, and Kerry jerked the shotgun up into position, took aim, and blew the pheasant out of the sky. The sound of the shot reverberated through the cornfield. The reporters following after Kerry could hardly believe what they had just seen: a presidential candidate blasting a bird with a shotgun. Kerry, of course, was making his point: he was an avid sportsman who had been hunting since he was 12—only a serious hunter would use a 12-gauge shotgun—who was also in favor of gun control. You don't need an Uzi to go bird-hunting, Kerry often said. Then, just as suddenly as he had flushed the first bird, Buck found a second. Kerry listened to the flapping of the pheasant's wings. No sooner had it cleared the thin line of horizon than Kerry, his 12-gauge brought back up to his shoulder, blew the second bird out of the sky, too.

5

IOWA

O n this cold winter day in Boston—Sunday, November 9—John Kerry had made sure that his public schedule ended in the late afternoon so he could be at his townhouse on Louisburg Square for a series of meetings that evening—meetings, he hoped, that might result in changing the direction of his floundering campaign.

In mid-October, not long after he had talked to Ted Kennedy on the floor of the Senate, Kerry ordered his campaign to commission the Mellman Group to conduct yet another poll of 500 likely voters in Iowa. These were people who had a history of participating on caucus night, not just names selected out of the telephone book. When the data from the poll came in, Kerry was encouraged, as he had been by previous internal polls in Iowa. Despite the New Hampshire polls, and despite the negative publicity coming from the national media, Kerry's poll numbers in Iowa remained promising. He had an impressive 69-percent-favorable approval rating (the highest favorable number of all the candidates) compared to only 12 percent unfavorable. Moreover, when he was surveyed with the rest of the field, Kerry did quite well. With the margin of error, the race was still a three-way dead heat: Dean 24, Kerry 21, Gephardt 21, Edwards 10, Clark 5, Lieberman 5, Kucinich 3, Braun 1, and Sharpton 0. Time after time, the numbers in these internal polls showed Kerry holding steady, which was heartening to him.

The problem with his campaign, Kerry had decided, was this: he could not concentrate on the job of being the candidate because he was constantly having to manage his bickering staff. Even with Lehane gone, Jordan and Shrum never stopped fighting; in fact, there was so much quarreling that Jordan had never been able to replace Lehane. As one insider put it at the time, the campaign was "poisonous, with constant backstabbing." But that wasn't the worst of it. The feuding of the Boston and Washington factions may have kept Kerry from mounting a concerted effort to lock in the support of key members of Congress necessary for him to win the nomination. Congressman Adam Smith of Washington had been helpful, and Kerry had enjoyed the early support of Congresswoman Carolyn Maloney of New York and Congressman Bill Pascrell of New Jersey, but members of both the House and the Senate appeared reluctant to endorse him. "It seemed [Kerry] was always refereeing his campaign," one confidant told a reporter. "He was forced into the machinations of the campaign, adjudicating disputes among his staff, consultants, colleagues in Congress, and schedulers—and so somebody who has very considerable talents and background wasn't able to be an optimal candidate." In fact, some members of Congress felt that if Kerry could not handle his own campaign staff during the primary season, how could he run a larger political or governmental organization?

As it happened, Kennedy was not the only one lobbying Kerry to get rid of Jordan. One person close to Teresa Heinz believed that she had urged her husband to replace Jordan after she and Jordan had had several arguments on the telephone. (The disputes sprung from Heinz's disappointment that Jordan had refused to begin airing ads in the summer as the Dean campaign was starting to build momentum.) It was never a secret that in the Jordan–Shrum feud Teresa favored Shrum, whom she considered a friend. Equally vocal in her dislike of Jordan was Jeanne Shaheen, who, once she signed on as national chairwoman in September, took over the day-to-day operation of the campaign. Within a month, it became obvious to Shaheen that Kerry needed to make a change. "It is perfectly clear to me that Jeanne Shaheen grabbed the Kerry campaign by the lapels sometime in October and shook it," Peter Burling, the Democrat state House minority leader in New Hampshire whose farmhouse Kerry had visited in January and made news by using the phrase "When I am president," told one newspaper. Armed with the opinions of those he trusted most—Kennedy, Shaheen, Teresa—urging him to act, Kerry knew he had to do something.

In the third week of October, Kerry asked McKean if there was any reason he could think of why he should not change campaign managers. McKean thought it over. No, there was no reason. The final decision—to replace Jordan—was made around Halloween, the day Kerry went pheasant-hunting. By November 1, Jordan had against him Kerry's family, Kerry's friends in Boston, the consultants in Washington, and a new group—the fund-raisers. They could not raise money, they said, because of the campaign's poor showing, which they now blamed on Jordan.

But Kerry had a problem: he didn't have a replacement for Jordan waiting in the wings. During the first week in November, Kerry talked to four different people to get their advice: his brother

Cameron; David McKean; John Sasso, a friend from Boston and Washington political circles and an adviser; and Michael Whouley, a political consultant who had known Kerry since 1982 when he had worked as a field director on Kerry's successful lieutenant-governor campaign. Kerry did not include Shrum in these discussions; he felt Shrum was too wrapped up in the conflict to be objective. Various names were mentioned, but, as of the evening of Thursday, November 8, Kerry still did not have a replacement. Of those advising him, Whouley was perhaps most vocal, and he was lobbying strongly for Mary Beth Cahill. Currently Kennedy's chief of staff, Cahill was someone Kerry had known for years from Massachusetts politics. He considered her a close and trusted friend. She was also David McKean's counterpart in the suite of offices down the hall from his own. Kerry was drawn to the idea of Cahill because she was indisputably competent—and because he liked her without hesitation.

On Friday morning, after a series of conversations, again with Cameron, Whouley, and Sasso—McKean had gone into the hospital that day for knee surgery—Kerry made up his mind to approach Cahill. A veteran of the Washington-based women's activist group Emily's List, where she had worked from 1993 until 1998, and the Clinton White House, where she had served as assistant to the president and director of public liaison from 1998 until Clinton left office in January of 2001, Cahill was, Kerry decided, a politically sophisticated, no-nonsense operative with an aggressive but efficient management style—just what he needed. The oldest of six children in a middle-class family in Boston, she had managed races in both the House and the Senate, including those of Senator Patrick Leahy of Vermont. Her one flaw was obvious: she had never before worked on a presidential campaign.

Nevertheless, Kerry called Kennedy on Friday morning to tell him he had decided to make a change and that the person he wanted to hire was *his* chief of staff. That was fine with him, Kennedy said. He was happy to contribute his chief of staff to Kerry's campaign effort. He was also flattered that, at this time of crisis, Kerry had reached out to Kennedy for help. President Kennedy had made Kerry dream of becoming president; now his brother—and the keeper of the Kennedy flame—was giving him the guidance, and the staff, that he needed to realize the dream. If Kerry wanted to hire Cahill, Kennedy said, he should give her a call.

That Friday night, Kerry phoned Cahill at home in Washington. "I want to make a change," he told her. "I think that this campaign has great promise, but, you know, there's a lot of infighting. I need for this to get straightened out. Will you help me?"

Earlier in the day, Kennedy had prepared Cahill that Kerry would be calling her to ask if she would be his campaign manager, so she knew what she was going to say to Kerry when the call came. "Let me talk to my husband," Cahill said. "I'll call you right back."

She called back almost immediately. She wanted Kerry to know that she would welcome the chance to be his campaign manager. "I'll be there on Monday morning," she said.

"That's great," Kerry said. "That's just great."

With Cahill lined up, Kerry called a meeting of his staff for early Sunday evening at the Boston townhouse. The stated reason for the meeting was to discuss media strategy.

When Jordan arrived at the townhouse, he had no idea that anything unusual was in the works. He had even met with a reporter on Friday in Washington to discuss the future of the campaign. If he'd been looking for them that Sunday, Jordan would have seen the signs, but he didn't. There were, for example, fewer staffers at the townhouse than there should have been for a media planning session. When Jordan came in, Kerry and Jeanne Shaheen took him into a separate room for a private meeting. Right off, Kerry told him he had decided to replace him as campaign manager. "I need to make a change to appease the backers," Kerry said. "They feel we're being outgunned by Dean."

Jordan was shocked. He couldn't believe what Kerry had just told him. Even though the campaign had been plagued by infighting for months, he never thought Kerry would fire him. Jordan's surprise quickly turned to anger. Kerry told him he would prefer for him to resign, but Jordan refused. If Kerry was going to get rid of him, Jordan said, he would have to fire him. So Kerry did. Press reports described the exchange as "tense." But Kerry had done what he had to do. Livid and hurt, Jordan stormed out of the townhouse in a huff. He was going back to Washington to tell the staff, almost all of whom he had hired, that he was no longer part of the campaign.

Kerry was not happy with the way the conversation had gone. He called David McKean in Washington to see if he would go over to the campaign headquarters, speak to the staff, and try to keep the situation calm, but McKean was recovering from his knee surgery. He was sitting in his living room, loaded up on painkillers, with his knee packed in ice. There was no way he could go to headquarters that night. Instead, Kerry sent Jim Margolis, one of his media advisers.

Margolis arranged a conference call with the staff in Washington so Kerry could personally tell them of his decision. Many staffers were shocked. Some lashed out at Kerry. They contended that he was the problem, not Jordan. Kerry tried to downplay the whole ordeal. During part of the one-hour call, which was conducted via speakerphone, he even ate dinner—which was a mistake: published reports used that detail to depict him as callous and uncaring in the way he handled the Jordan firing. As he conducted the call, Kerry also addressed concerns that Shrum was behind the move, since Shrum and Cahill were friends. Shrum had nothing to do with his decision to replace Jordan, Kerry said. Toward the end of the often-contentious call, Kerry cut to the bottom line. "We're doing well," he said, "but nobody's hearing it. We're not breaking through. We need to do something to shake things up and make people look at us again."

Early Monday morning, Kerry sent out an e-mail blast announcing his decision to change campaign managers. Not surprisingly, there was fallout from the firing. Two senior staffers—Robert Gibbs, the campaign press secretary, and Carl Chidlow, the deputy finance director—quit. Kerry brought in David Morehouse, who had worked for Gore in 2000, to help in the area of communications. If there was chaos—and there was—it was temporary. On Monday morning, Cahill arrived for work at the campaign's headquarters, a modest townhouse in a residential neighborhood near the Capitol. She took charge right away, as Kerry had known she would, assembling the staff in order to speak to them all at once.

"Jim Jordan is a talented man and a good leader," she told the group of 100, many of them loyal to Jordan, "but John has made a change. No one is going to be fired. I hope very much that you all are going to stay, because I've heard so many good things about how talented you are. But if you're going to leave, I want you to leave now." There was too much to do, Cahill said, to have to worry about personnel issues going forward. She also did not want the campaign subjected to a daily grind of negative publicity. She preferred to get all the bad news out at the start. No one else left.

On Tuesday, *The New York Times* ran a front-page story about the Jordan firing—the paper presented the story for what it was, major news in the political world—and suggested there might even be something called "the Shrum curse" that was destroying the Kerry campaign the same way it had wrecked Gore's campaign in 2000. Curse or no curse, Cahill had to get on with her job. Her first move was to fill Gibbs's position with Stephanie Cutter, who was currently press spokesperson for Ted Kennedy. She also hired Michael Meehan and David DeMartino to work in the communications department. Chidlow's duties would be absorbed by the general fund-raising staff. "I also sat down and had one-on-one meetings with most of the staff people," Mary Beth Cahill says. "By and large, they were very welcoming. They were happy to have the time of turmoil over. They felt very strong respect and affection for Jim Jordan, but they were there for John Kerry."

What also became obvious right away was Cahill's management style. Confident and sure-handed, Cahill did not hesitate to make decisions, and those decisions were based on one overriding dictum: whatever she did had to be in the best interest of the campaign. About this, Kerry had never had any doubts. He had known her for so long through the world of Massachusetts politics he had no doubt she would do what she was doing right now—taking charge and making decisions—which was why he had offered her the job without ever even having her sit for an interview.

As a way to show that the staff shake-up was a new beginning and not the next step in a meltdown, the campaign began to run a television ad that was more pointed and aggressive than any they had aired so far. It showed Bush walking across the flight deck of the *Abraham Lincoln* on the day he made his "mission accomplished" speech. As Bush smiles at the camera, an announcer asks, "Who can take on George Bush and change the direction of the nation?" The implied answer, of course, was John Kerry.

Kerry was realistic, almost philosophical, about the decisions he had made. "We needed a change in leadership," he told the journalist Meryl Gordon at the time. "[Mary Beth] knows all the players, all the people who are working with me." As for the departure of Gibbs and Chidlow, he said, "I knew there would be fallout and a downside, but the upside is yet to come." Kerry adds: "There was obviously a difficult moment when I knew it wasn't working and I had to make a change. That was hard because I knew I would take a hit. But I knew in my heart and my gut I couldn't make happen the things I knew had to happen in order to win. But I always felt we could win."

Still, Kerry knew that it wasn't enough just to replace his campaign manager. He needed to revamp his stump speech and alter his campaign style, too. Kennedy's suggested "Phil Donahue approach" had worked well for Elizabeth Dole, one of the stiffest speakers in politics, when she ventured out into the audience at the Republican National Convention in 1996 to introduce her husband, then running for president. She would deliver passages of a speech, then segue into chats with people in the audience. The style made her seem friendly and relaxed; maybe the same could work with Kerry. Shaheen agreed that Kerry's approach needed to be less studied, more spontaneous. He had a brilliant wit, which was not coming through in his public appearances. Cahill, too, wanted to make changes—a shorter, punchier stump speech, for one. She also didn't like the slogan "The Courage to Do What's Right for America."

With all of these changes in the works, Kerry felt hopeful as he returned to Iowa for the Jefferson Jackson Dinner. That was the event, the campaign had decided, at which they would roll out Kerry's new look. Over the course of the week leading up to the dinner, Kerry read the galleys of *Tour of Duty*, Douglas Brinkley's book about Kerry's experiences in Vietnam and the antiwar movement. In mid-November, around the time galleys of the book had been sent out to publications for review, the December *Atlantic Monthly* had hit newsstands, and the cover article was an excerpt from Brinkley's forthcoming book. Many of the excerpted passages, which had been chosen by the magazine's editors, were graphically violent, but the book itself offered a more complete and balanced chronicle of what happened to Kerry both before and after his time in Vietnam.

On Friday, as he was preparing for his appearance at the Jefferson Jackson Dinner the next night, Kerry announced that he was going to reject public financing of his campaign. He had little choice: within the past week, Dean, who could raise far more money over the Internet than he could get from accepting federal matching funds, had decided to forgo public financing and raise his campaign money himself. Dean was rejecting $19 million, but now he was free to ignore the $45 million spending cap for the primary season and raise as much money as he could. He made his decision based on the assumption that he would win the nomination and have to run ads to counter an anticipated all-out attack by Bush, who himself had opted out of the federal matching-funds program and intended to amass an unheard-of $180 million, which had to be spent before the general election, when he was expected to accept federal matching funds totalling $75 million.

To remain competitive during the primaries, Kerry had to follow Dean's lead. But because his ability to raise money had dried up considerably, Kerry would have to put his own money into the campaign—as much as $8 million. In explaining his decision, Kerry told reporters in Des Moines, "I don't know what I'll put in because it depends on what people do in responding to this campaign. But I'm not going to fight with one hand tied behind my back. I don't believe in unilateral disarmament." Kerry started the impromptu press conference outside a diner at a campaign stop by making a candid assessment of his week. "As you all know," he said, "this has not been the easiest week in our campaign, but I've been in a lot of tough fights before and I've fought back and I've won." It was now that Kerry started calling himself the underdog. He also began saying that, to win, he would have to fight "for every single vote."

That night, Kerry received an e-mail message from a Seattle political columnist. "At the end of a difficult week," it read, "I suggest you remember a quote from Tom Pettit of NBC News on *The Today Show* after George H. W. Bush won the 1980 Iowa caucus. 'I would like to suggest that Ronald Reagan is politically dead.' A few days later, the Gipper fired campaign manager John Sears, prompting a new raft of similar stories on turmoil in his campaign. The rest, as they say, was history."

On Saturday night, as Kerry spoke at the Jefferson Jackson Dinner, the changes of the past week came together. The speech was well received; his stage presence was much improved. He liked his new slogan too: The Real Deal. His new ad campaign, especially the one showing Bush on the *Abraham Lincoln*, was sending a message as well: he was willing to take on Bush, even if that meant engaging in smashmouth politics. By the night of the dinner, Cahill had begun to formulate her overall strategy for the campaign. The polls continued to show Kerry doing badly in New Hampshire but much better in Iowa than the media was reporting, so Cahill reached the potentially risky decision to pull all the staff from around the country—from New Hampshire, South Carolina, Washington state, Washington, D.C.—and make Iowa the focus of the campaign from now until Caucus Day in January.

To do this, Cahill had to relocate as many as 100 campaign workers from New Hampshire alone. If the campaign failed in Iowa, Kerry would not have enough time to recover in New Hampshire, or in South Carolina, which had been used as a firewall by candidates who had not done as well as they would have liked in Iowa or New Hampshire. Cahill was gambling everything on Iowa. Should Kerry win, however, the bounce he would get could propel him to victory in New Hampshire and beyond. Tad Devine, Shrum's business partner, gave Cahill's plan a name: the "slingshot" strategy. Win Iowa, and Kerry would be launched to more victories, like a rock flung out of a slingshot.

To guarantee that her slingshot strategy would work, Cahill imported the man from Boston who had lobbied for her to get the job, Michael Whouley. Whouley had a reputation as one of the best field-operations managers in the business, which was why Clinton had used him in 1992 and Gore had done the same in 2000. If Whouley couldn't get people to show up and caucus for Kerry in Iowa, it couldn't be done.

A week later, on November 21, Kerry implemented another of Cahill's ideas. At Concord High School in Concord, New Hampshire—in one of the last appearances he would make in the state before concentrating almost entirely on Iowa—Kerry made a speech in which he announced what he would do, if he became president, during his first 100 days in office. First, he would sign an executive order banning ex–government officials from becoming lob-byists; second, he would decrease the United States' dependence on Middle East oil through conservation and the development of new sources of energy; third, he would "change the corporate culture" in America by vigorously prosecuting executive officers accused of wrongdoing; and fourth, he would "roll back George Bush's assault on the environment." The speech was a good move because it allowed Kerry a forum in which to describe the issues that were important to him. At the end of the day in New Hampshire, during which he spent most of his time on the Real Deal Express, the name the campaign had given the bus in which he now traveled, Kerry went to a firehouse for a chili feed. This type of event—down-home, relaxed, blue-collar—the campaign hoped, would become, as *The New York Times* described it, "his signature stop."

At the same time that Kerry's campaign was undergoing a complete makeover, Dean was having problems of his own. The Jewish community had never forgiven the comments he had made in Santa Fe, especially since he had also equated Hamas terrorists with "sol-diers." In early November, Dean said that he wanted to be "the candidate for guys with Confederate flags in their pickup trucks." Forget that the Confederate flag, as a symbol, was offensive to millions of voters in America. Dean didn't even grasp that it was patronizing for a rich and privileged WASP from Park Avenue, boarding school, and Yale to make such a comment. If he had ever had the chance, no matter how remote, of getting the votes of those pickup-truck-owning Southerners, he'd blown it now. What's more, he had also lost the support of those voters who would be offended by his willingness to speak well of the Confederate flag—potentially a much larger group. However, Dean's increasingly aberrant behavior did not keep the Service Employees International Union and the American Federation of

State, County, and Municipal Employees from endorsing him in mid-November.

On Saturday, November 22, *The New York Times* ran a story documenting how Dean had avoided the draft as a young man. In 1970, he went to his draft physical with a set of X-rays and a letter from his personal doctor. "It was like a scene from the movie *Alice's Restaurant*," the paper quoted Dean as saying. Specifically, Dean's doctor argued that because Dean suffered from spondylolysis, a condition that produces lower-back pain that can radiate down both legs, he should be given a medical deferment. The military doctor agreed and granted Dean a 1Y deferment, which replaced the 2S deferment he'd had as a Yale undergraduate. With a 1Y, Dean could be drafted only under dire circumstances. This story galled Kerry, the decorated veteran. On Sunday, the Kerry campaign issued a press release that quoted Max Cleland as saying, "At a time when young Americans are being killed and wounded by President Bush's failed policy in Iraq, we don't need another governor who ran from going to Vietnam leading our country. We cannot afford to have a leader who weaseled out of going to Vietnam on a medical deferment for a bad back and wound up on the ski slopes of Aspen like Howard Dean." Cleland's charge turned out to be true: while Dean had maintained his medical deferment based on a lower-back disorder, he was known to go skiing in Colorado.

On Monday, the 24th, Dean was on the defensive. At a debate in Des Moines, he was the target of attacks by Kerry and Gephardt. Kerry was participating from Washington, where he was preparing to cast a vote to block Bush's proposed Medicare bill, so while the other candidates appeared onstage in Iowa, Kerry was being beamed in on an oversized flat-screen monitor positioned on the stage with them. Because of the impending vote, Medicare—and social services in general—was a focus of the debate. At one point, Dean said he would reduce the growth of Medicare and cut social-services programs. Gephardt lambasted Dean for this, contending, "We didn't cut the most vulnerable, as he did in Vermont. He cut Medicaid. He cut the prescription-drug program. He cut funding for the blind and the disabled. Now, I have a different version of how to do this. And I think that's what we did in the middle nineties at the federal level. We got the budget in balance."

Dean was aggravated by Gephardt's criticism. "I most certainly appreciate all this attention I'm getting," he said.

Then, from his flat-screen television, Kerry chimed in, pounding at Dean again and again over why he refused to promise not to slow the growth of the Medicare budget.

"Are you going to slow the rate of growth, Governor? Yes or no?" Kerry demanded.

"We are going to do what we have to do to make sure that Medicare lasts," Dean said, dodging the question.

"Are you going to slow the rate of growth, Governor—because that's a cut," Kerry roared.

"Well, I'd like to slow the rate of growth of this debate if I could," Dean said, trying to make light of what was becoming an unpleasant situation for him.

In December, Kerry began airing an ad in Iowa featuring Del Sandusky, who had been his chief petty officer on PCF 94. In the ad, Sandusky said that Kerry had "made decisions that saved our lives." He concluded by declaring, "This is a good American." The Sandusky ad was yet another step in the revitalization process of the Kerry campaign being carried out by Mary Beth Cahill, a process that now seemed to be working. On December 1, there was more evidence that Kerry's fortunes were turning around when the campaign announced, because of a surge of support following the Jefferson Jackson Dinner, that Kerry now had twenty-three state legislators pledged to him—a number that proved Kerry was amassing vital grassroots support among Iowans, if not the national media, which was still doting on Dean.

If the media was looking for something that would confirm Dean as the unstoppable presumed nominee, they got it on a chilly day in Harlem in New York City. On the morning of December 9, not quite one year after Al Gore had announced he would not run for president in 2004, he finally endorsed a candidate. "We need to re-make the Democratic Party," Gore told a small audience as the national press corps looked on. "We need to take it back on behalf of the people of this country. So I'm very proud and honored to endorse Howard Dean to be the next president of the United States."

Dean had briefly introduced Gore, as they appeared together at the National Black Theater's Institute for Action Arts, by saying that when his campaign set up the event he had "absolutely no idea that we were going to have the elected president of the United States here with us today"—a quip that got a rise from the audience. In Gore's opinion, Dean was the candidate to run against Bush, because he "was the only major candidate who made the correct judgment about the Iraq war" and because "he had the insight and courage to say and do the right thing." Gore added: "It was Osama bin Laden that attacked us, not Saddam Hussein. . . . [I]t was a mistake to get us into a quagmire over there." Gore finished by declaring, "I have come to the conclusion that in a field of great candidates, one candidate clearly now stands out. And so I'm asking all of you to join in this grassroots movement to elect Howard Dean President of the United States."

The media could hardly control itself. On CNN, Donna Brazile, Gore's campaign manager in 2000 and a commentator for the news network, encouraged the other candidates ("they know who they are") to drop out of the race. "Howard Dean has money, momentum, he has people," she said, "and now, with Al Gore's support, Howard Dean will be able to take his campaign across this country." On PBS, Adam Nagourney, the chief political reporter for *The New York Times*, told the network's Gwen Ifill that the Gore endorsement had remedied "what has been one of Howard Dean's biggest problems, which is that people just don't take him seriously as a real electable establishment Democrat." In fact, Nagourney said, "it's hard to see how anyone could overcome" the support for Dean in New Hampshire. CBS News was equally agog. After saying that "the coveted endorsement by Gore is a breathtaking victory for Dean," it quoted one Washington consultant, Dean Strother, who declared, "What this says is that all these Washington insiders who have been gnashing their teeth, wringing their hands, and clinging to their cocktail cups can relax now. Dean's been knighted by the ultimate insider. It's game, set, and match. It's over."

Actually, there were forty-one days to go before a vote would be cast in the first caucus, and as Dean, Gore, and the media were basking in their mutually reflected glory, Joe Lieberman had his own opinion of the Gore endorsement. Because Lieberman had been Gore's running mate in 2000, Lieberman had made the unusual move of saying he would not run against Gore should Gore choose to get into the race (he waited for Gore to announce a decision before he declared his own intentions), but Gore had not even bothered to contact Lieberman before making his surprise endorsement of Dean. Appearing on *The Today Show*, Lieberman said, "I was caught completely off guard." What really disturbed him, he said, "is that Al is supporting a candidate who is so fundamentally opposed to the basic transformation that Bill Clinton brought to this party in 1992." Did Lieberman think Gore was a loyal person, considering his actions? "I'm not going to talk about Al Gore's sense of loyalty this morning," Lieberman said flatly. His silence could not have been more damning.

On Thursday, December 11, Kerry turned 60. As he had watched the events of the last forty-eight hours unfold, he began to believe that the Gore endorsement might not be such a coup for Dean after all. Voters might dismiss Gore because he looked as if he were climbing on a bandwagon—after stabbing his former running mate in the back.

Then, as Caucus Day approached, everything changed. In the early morning hours of Saturday, December 13, reports began to come out of Iraq that Saddam Hussein had been captured. For months, speculation had swirled through the military, intelligence, and journalistic communities about Saddam. Some reports suggested he had been killed on the night military action began in Iraq. These reports said he had been blown up when bunker-buster bombs hit his underground hideaway in Baghdad. Soon the reports were discounted by sources in Washington and the Middle East and replaced by the theory that Saddam survived the initial strike on Baghdad and had fled to the region of the country where he had been born. As it happened, he had been found by a U.S. serviceman while he hid in a "spider hole"—a deep, concealed pit—next to a ramshackle lean-to near Tikrit, the village of his boyhood.

That night in Davenport, Kerry, in keeping with his new style— the short stump speech followed by an excursion à la Phil Donahue into the audience to field questions—announced he was going to stay until he had convinced all of the undecided voters in the room to vote for him. He ended up answering questions for one hour and forty-five minutes. Naturally, the capture of Saddam had been a topic of discussion. Kerry knew that this event could have a profound effect on the race, since Dean's candidacy was based so heavily on his anti-war message. The capture of Saddam reminded voters that Bush had taken the actions he had for a reason. Kerry disagreed with the direction Bush was taking the war, but he was convinced that Saddam was a threat to the people of Iraq, the region, and maybe even the world, which was why he had voted for Bush's war resolution.

On the evening of Sunday, December 14, Kerry held a forum with undecided voters that was broadcast on seven key television stations in Iowa and paid for by the campaign. The 30-minute show was an attempt by Kerry, in the tradition of Ross Perot, to get his message to the public without having to go through the filter of the media. The telecast, which cost $28,000, was overshadowed by the massive news coverage of the capture of Saddam, although that did not necessarily hurt Kerry. Dean, however, was hurt by a comment he made in Los Angeles the next night as he was giving what was billed as a major foreign-policy speech. "The capture of Saddam has not made America safer," Dean said, asserting that Saddam was not a part of the worldwide terrorist network that was the target of Bush's war on terrorism.

By Tuesday, December 16, the national press was beginning to realize that the Kerry campaign was in a turnaround. "In the last five weeks," David Halbfinger wrote in *The New York Times*, "[Kerry] has shaken up his staff, shortened and sharpened his stump speech, replaced his slogan—dropping the 'courage to do what's right' for a 'real deal' for America—and started trumpeting what he would do in the first 100 days if elected president." At this time, Kerry lent the campaign $850,000 of his own money (from personal credit at his bank) and took the first steps toward borrowing against the equity of the townhouse in Boston that he owned with Teresa—a critical and immediate cash infusion that would come within the next week or so. (Technically, the townhouse was owned by a trust, so the money would be borrowed by the trust, a method that Kerry had used before.) "This is a clear statement by John Kerry," Mary Beth Cahill said to the press that day, referring to the infusion of private money. "He is in the race to win the nomination and defeat George Bush."

As this was happening, Dean blundered yet again while addressing an audience in New Hampshire. "The only way to have a Jewish democracy is to get out of the West Bank at some point," he said. "It's a Jewish state, it's not a democracy." It seemed incomprehensible that Dean did not know Israel was a democracy, not to mention the only American ally in the region, so he must have been making a political statement. If so, his point was unclear (at best) or disturbing (at worst). He was either disingenuous or anti-Israel.

While Dean struggled, the Kerry campaign was about to surge. On December 22, Kerry set out on a 24-hour campaign swing through Iowa on the Real Deal Express. By Friday of that week, he had secured the mortgage on his house, a loan that totalled $6.5 million. The dual unfolding stories—Kerry's rise in popularity as Dean became gaffe-prone—seemed to have no effect on fund-raising. For while Kerry was having to put his own money into his campaign, by the end of December Dean had raised more than $40 million, a sum made even more impressive by the fact that most of it had come in the form of individual contributions over the Internet.

This was why conventional wisdom suggested that Dean was still the candidate to beat. As Adam Nagourney put it in the *Times* on Monday, December 29, sounding a much different note than his paper had only days before when it documented the Kerry turnaround, "The consensus in Democratic circles is that the prolonged holiday blackout has frozen the race in place. That is good news for Dr. Dean, who most polls show is far ahead in New Hampshire and in a strong position here [in Iowa]." That was not the general feeling among those Democrats who attended a New Year's Eve party thrown by the Kerry campaign at the Sioux City Community Theater. There, the sense of what was happening was that there would be a three-way race between Kerry, Dean, and Gephardt, as the Kerry internal polls had been suggesting for weeks. (Edwards was still far back in the pack.) If the race in Iowa did come down to a three-way slugfest, anyone could win on Caucus Night.

As the new year began, the other candidates continued to attack Dean. On Sunday, January 4, at a debate in Johnston, Iowa, Lieberman challenged him on a variety of topics, among them tax cuts and Iraq. "I don't know how anybody could say," Lieberman declared about the capture of Saddam Hussein, "that we're not safer with a homicidal maniac, a brutal dictator, an enemy of the United States, a supporter of terrorism . . . in prison instead of in power." He also criticized Dean for his decision to keep sealed certain records of his tenure as governor of Vermont. At one point, Lieberman offered Dean a pen and asked him to sign a document releasing the papers. Dean refused, which made him look as if he had something to hide, even if he didn't. The exchanges between Lieberman and Dean became so intense during the debate that the moderator, Paul Anger, the editor of *The Des Moines Register,* finally suggested that the two men "take it outside."

But, on Monday, January 5, Dean got yet another boost from the media when both *Time* and *Newsweek* put him on their covers in the same week. The general sense among the press was that, despite his mistakes, Dean had the nomination sewn up. If journalists had access to the Kerry campaign's internal polls in Iowa, which showed that he was still doing well, they were not writing about them. Then again, they were only reflecting what most pundits and opinion-makers felt as well: that Dean would win in Iowa, win in a land-slide in New Hampshire, and roll on easily to the nomination. These observers pointed to the national polls and Dean's huge war chest of cash. "The debate," Deborah Orin wrote in the *New York Post* about the January 4 forum, "offered one of the final chances to change the dynamics—and Team Dean is grinning big-time be-cause that didn't happen. Democratic rivals are trying to make an issue of Dean's hot temper and shoot-from-the-hip gaffes, but he stayed cool and didn't rise to the bait—so the debate script played perfectly for him."

On January 7, Douglas Brinkley appeared on *The Today Show* with Katie Couric and on *The O'Reilly Factor* with Bill O'Reilly to promote *Tour of Duty,* which became a staple of the campaign; many fans were asking Kerry and the members of his Vietnam navy crews who traveled with him to sign their books. Brinkley's book gave the veterans a new relevance, and it soon hit *The New York Times* best-seller list. Meanwhile, the Dean campaign wasn't faring so well. The Gore endorsement had not been the clincher that the pundits had predicted it would be. As Kerry had privately noted, in many ways the endorsement had backfired. Lieberman came to be seen as an injured party, and Gore was viewed as a crass opportunist who had betrayed a loyal friend.

What was really happening between the Kerry and Dean camps could be seen in the public appearances of the two candidates. Kerry was growing more relaxed and open before audiences. On Saturday, January 10, after he had been introduced at a rally in Dubuque by Ted Kennedy, Kerry joked with the crowd, saying, "I was standing out there, and I was asked, 'Is it hard to live in the shadow of a great senator like Ted Kennedy? Is it upsetting to you personally to know that you will never have a legislative record as dazzling as Ted Kennedy? Are you jealous of the fact that you have to live with a living legend like him?' " Kerry paused for his punch line. "And, it was *Teddy* asking me the questions," he said. The crowd roared.

The following evening, when a Republican heckler stood up in a question-and-answer session in Oelwein, Iowa, and described Dean as being "pompous" and "mean-mouthing," Dean started to speak and the man interrupted him. "You sit down!" Dean shouted, red-faced. "You had your say! Now I'm going to have my say!" It was an unpleasant display. Some observers felt that Dean had not recovered from the incident when, later that day, he participated in a debate sponsored by the Iowa Black and Brown Presidential Forum, an orginization that advanced minority causes—and performed badly.

While Dean was making miscues, his campaign began running a new series of attack ads that singled out Dean's Democratic opponents, a move that broke an unspoken rule in politics: attack candidates in your party at your own risk. The Dean staffers must have been worried about the strength of the Kerry and Gephardt campaigns, for those candidates were Dean's targets—but almost from the moment they hit the airwaves, there were negative repercussions. It got so bad so quickly that the Dean campaign announced they were pulling the ads. (The ads, however, still ran in some cities right up until Caucus Day.)

In the middle of what was quickly becoming a free-for-all, the candidates showed up on the evening of Sunday, January 11, for the last debate to be held before the caucuses, now one week away. It was at this debate that Al Sharpton scored several devastating hits on Dean. "It seems as though you just discovered blacks and browns during this campaign," Sharpton said to Dean at one point. Dean tried to fight back by arguing that he had hired African-American and Latino staffers while he was governor of Vermont, but Sharpton did not let up. Sharpton's charge was this: in twelve years as Vermont governor, Dean had never appointed a black or Hispanic cabinet member. As Sharpton pounded away, Dean, frustrated by the exchange, had to admit that the claim was true. Dean seemed rattled, unfocused. But he had no time to recover before Sharpton hit him again, saying, "If you want to lecture people on race, you ought to have the background and track record in order to do that. . . . Governors import talent. Governors reach all over the country to make sure they have diversity." In a feeble attempt to regain some position on the issue, Dean listed his African-American and Latino supporters, adding, "I will take a backseat to no one in my commitment to civil rights." But Sharpton's charges had hit home.

"Al Sharpton was given several alternative approaches of how you might go after Dean," says Roger Stone, a political consultant who was informally advising Sharpton at the time, "and that approach"— criticizing Dean for the absence of minorities in his cabinet—"was the one that he selected. I think most of that advice actually came from Charles Halloran, his campaign manager." But Sharpton had taken Stone's advice on other occasions. "There were times where I was gritting my teeth because I suggested things that he could do that he didn't do. There were other times when you mentioned something very casually in conversation, and then, you know, he was using it on TV a week later. I gave him a lot of advice—some of it he chose to accept; some of it he chose to ignore."

Being a target for attacks came with being a frontrunner, and, according to the latest Zogby poll, Dean was still in the lead with 25 percent; Gephardt had 23, Kerry 15, Edwards 14, Clark 3, and Lieberman 3. The Zogby poll differed significantly from the internal polling numbers the Kerry campaign was seeing. What Zogby also didn't explain was why there were so many undecided voters—17 percent—in a race with so many candidates. That number should have suggested a race that was still wide open.

For months, Kerry had been saying that the race would be won or lost not in the weeks before Labor Day but in the final days of the campaign. With only a handful of days left before Caucus Day, the campaign was in the homestretch. As it turned out, few if any campaigns would ever have the kind of homestretch run that the Kerry campaign would have.

With only four days left before the caucuses, Kerry left the Real Deal Express behind and took to the air to reach the territory he felt he needed to cover. At 9 a.m. at the airport in Council Bluffs, Kerry climbed into the cockpit of a helicopter beside the pilot. Because of the craft's size, Kerry was joined only by a staffer and three reporters. When the helicopter took off, Kerry shouted, "Rock and roll!" Then, as the pilot guided the craft into the sky, Kerry said, "If you're game, I'd like to fly it a bit at some point." Of course, that was another reason for the flight: Kerry, who loved any activity with a sense of adventure to it—skiing, windsurfing, hang-gliding—wanted to fly the helicopter as well. It wouldn't hurt that the photograph to be picked up by the press on the Friday before the caucus would show him—sure of himself, steady-handed, in control—piloting a helicopter. The caption could write itself: The Kerry campaign was flying high. And it *was*, too. The night before, in Des Moines, at a jam-packed event for undecided voters, Kerry took questions for nearly two hours. "We're staying here till the sun rises," he warned the audience, "until we get you to agree"—to vote for him, that is. Periodically, Kerry would ask for a show of hands to see how many people were still undecided. He kept taking questions and polling the audience, with fewer and fewer raising their hands each time, until almost nobody was left in doubt. Kerry simply wore down the undecided voters in the room.

Kerry didn't pilot the helicopter on that first flight, to Carroll—where he met with a group of thirty-five undecided voters in the home of a local family—but he did take the controls on the flight from Carroll to Sioux City. He also piloted part of the trip from Sioux City to Adel, but handed over the controls for the last leg to Fort Dodge, sleeping most of the way. Kerry was campaigning hard, encouraged by new public polls, one of which, released to reporters on Thursday for publication on Friday, put Kerry in the lead, with a breakdown of Kerry 22, Dean 21, Gephardt 21, and Edwards 17. Perhaps that was why Tom Harkin, who had endorsed Dean early, now implored Dean to pull his negative ads once and for all—or lose to Kerry. Harkin also suggested that Dean needed to soften his image by wearing a sweater instead of the cheap suit he was known to wear for days on end. So, on Thursday, there Dean was—in a handsome pullover sweater. Dean told a reporter, "I would never not want to follow Senator Harkin's advice."

On Friday, part of the strategy behind Kerry's trip in the helicopter appeared in the pages of newspapers across the state. Along with the daily story about Kerry was a photo of him wearing a winter coat and a radio headset as he flew the helicopter. Kerry had made fun of Bush for "playing dress-up" and landing on the deck of an aircraft carrier; now here he was—actually flying a helicopter, a real pilot, the real deal. Even more noteworthy, on Friday, *The New York Times* reported that Kerry was "suddenly being taken seriously as a potential winner of the Iowa caucuses for the first time in months."

Meanwhile, Dean followed Harkin's advice and pulled his negative ads, although some still ran in certain markets, and replaced them with an ad gently questioning Kerry's reluctance to support farm subsidies. Dean also appeared in his pullover sweater for a second day, faintly suggesting that he was taking fashion advice in the same way that Al Gore had when he changed his wardrobe to earth tones to look more manly. Surely, in the final push, voters were not going to decide to vote for Dean based on whether he was wearing a suit or a sweater, but Dean was still careful to follow Harkin's advice. "Dr. Dean, the former governor of Vermont," *The Times* observed, "spent a second consecutive day campaigning in a soft crewneck sweater, instead of his usual suit and tie, leading an unwieldy caravan of 13 vehicles, 55 reporters, a portable wireless Internet hub, assorted staff, political celebrities, and enough food to feed them across 631 miles since Thursday."

Another Dean campaign tactic was called the Perfect Storm. From across the country, 3,500 volunteers had traveled to Iowa however they could—by bus, airplane, car, van—to put on orange toboggans and go door-to-door to explain to Iowans why they were supporting Dean. This was supposed to represent the ultimate example of grassroots support. The Deaniacs were going to fan out across the state, like the perfect storm, and persuade the citizens of Iowa to vote for their man.

The race, according to Dean, was now "deadlocked." Going into the final weekend, Kerry was continuing to rise in the polls, Dean was continuing to drop, and Gephardt refused to pull his ad attacking Dean for downsizing the Medicare program in Vermont when he was governor. Dean had become so rattled that he had all but stopped holding events where he would have to interact with the audience. For his part, Kerry couldn't hold enough events where he got to meet people—venue after venue now saw overflow crowds—and at those events, he spent time talking directly to undecided voters. Kerry decided to wrap up his ad buy with a commercial featuring the wife of the popular Iowa governor, Christie Vilsack, who reassured her fellow Iowans that "he'll fight for us." Kerry hoped that this ad, along with two more solid days of nonstop campaigning, might put him in a position to win on Monday night. But what was about to happen in the final forty-eight hours of the campaign no one could have foreseen—not Kerry's staff, not his family or friends, not even Kerry himself.

Earlier in the week, Jim Rassmann, a retired Los Angeles County sheriff's deputy living in Florence, Oregon, was walking through a bookstore in Glendale, California, where he and his wife were visiting her family, when he spotted a copy of *Tour of Duty*. Rassmann picked up the book, flipped through the pages, and noticed that he was mentioned in it, even though he had not been interviewed. (He would find out later that Brinkley had tried to reach him but had searched for his name spelled with one "n" instead of two.) Rassmann was not completely surprised at seeing his name in the book, because he had had an encounter with Kerry on the Mekong Delta in the spring of 1969 that he would never forget.

On March 13, 1969, Rassmann, a Green Beret and Special Forces lieutenant, was traveling on the Bay Hap River on PCF 94, a swift boat that Kerry was commanding. They were the lead boat in a caravan of swift boats returning from a mission up the river when they were caught in a sudden ambush. Land mines exploded in the river as machine-gun fire rang out from both shores. Kerry, thrown into the bulkhead by an explosion, was wounded in the arm. "I was seated with one foot outside the hatch on the right-hand side of the boat," Jim Rassmann says, "and my left on the other side, and I was eating chocolate-chip cookies. Somebody had gotten a CARE package, and I was starving, so I was eating chocolate-chip cookies. And then the boat to our left had a mine go off under it. Whatever blew me off the boat was what threw John across the pilothouse and wounded him."

"Man overboard!" Del Sandusky yelled, but Kerry did not hear him. Weighted down with gear, Rassmann sank to the bottom of the river, where he struggled to abandon the gear. By the time Rassmann had freed himself of the equipment and resurfaced, Kerry's boat had moved on toward the boat that had been blown out of the water and away from the continuing enemy attack. "When I came up, the boat was gone," Rassmann says. "Right away, I started getting shot at, so I went back under to the bottom of the river. I did this over and over. About the fifth or sixth time I came up for air I figured my goose was cooked because if I got to shore without getting hit they were going to kill me. It looked like the boats had left me, too."

Then Rassmann looked downriver and saw the boats coming back. Kerry had realized that Rassmann was missing, so he'd turned the boats around to come back for him. "Kerry was in the lead boat," Rassmann says. "When it got there, I grabbed hold of the bow and started climbing up. But I got to the edge and couldn't get over, and that's when John came to pull me aboard. I expected him to get hit at any second, because there was so much fire. I couldn't believe that *I* hadn't been hit." With David Alston supplying suppressing fire, Kerry leaned over, extended his wounded arm, and pulled Rassmann onto the boat. For saving Rassmann, Kerry would receive the Bronze Star with Combat "V." The medal citation described Kerry's actions: "The man was receiving sniper fire from both banks. Lt. Kerry directed his gunners to provide suppressing fire, while from an exposed position on the bow, his arm bleeding and in pain, with disregard for his personal safety, he pulled the man aboard. . . . Lt. Kerry's calmness, professionalism and great personal courage under fire were in keeping with the highest traditions of the United States Naval Service."

As he turned the pages of Brinkley's book, Rassmann was brought back to that day on the Mekong Delta and began to cry uncontrollably in the middle of the bookstore. Suddenly he put the book down. "I have to go," he told his wife and rushed outside to their car.

Back home in Oregon on Friday, three days before the Iowa caucus, Rassmann picked up the phone and called the Washington headquarters of John Kerry for President. The phone could have been answered by a volunteer, who may or may not have understood the importance of the call, but fortunately it was answered by Jackie Williams, the most senior of the paid staff in charge of answering the phones and overseeing the volunteers who helped them.

"My name is Jim Rassmann," he told Williams. "I served with John Kerry in Vietnam, and I was wondering if there was anything

I could do to help. I saw that John is in another tough fight, and I want to lend a hand."

Williams took Rassmann's name and telephone number and told him someone would call him back. She immediately passed on Rassmann's information to John Hurley, Kerry's staffer who dealt with veterans issues. Hurley recognized Rassmann's name instantly, called him in Oregon, and asked him if he would be willing to fly to Iowa to be reunited with Kerry. Rassmann readily agreed. He was on a flight the next morning—Saturday, two days before Caucus Day.

Naturally, Kerry had a full day of campaigning planned, and none of the events had been scheduled around veterans issues, even though for weeks now Kerry had kept a group of Vietnam veterans at his side. The best that the campaign could do at the last minute was to reunite Rassmann with Kerry at an event that was to take place at the Creative Visions Human Development Center in Des Moines. The location and the event were not ideal. The facility was a women's health clinic, and the event was meant to honor young up-and-coming African-American leaders in Iowa, a state not known for its minority population. Kerry was also supposed to be endorsed at the event by a key member of the Des Moines city council. Now, with no explanation whatsoever, there would also be a reunion of two veterans who had not seen each other in thirty-five years. There was one additional problem: the reunion had been set up for 4:15 in the afternoon, a media alert had already been sent out, Rassmann was on his way to Des Moines, but no one had told Kerry about any of this. He didn't even know that Rassmann had phoned the Washington headquarters, much less that the two of them were about to be reunited.

Finally, David Wade realized that Kerry hadn't been told, so he phoned Del Sandusky, who was traveling with the campaign, filled him in on what was happening, and asked him to tell Kerry at once. When Sandusky informed Kerry, who was en route to Des Moines from Davenport, Kerry couldn't believe it. He hadn't seen Rassmann in three and a half decades.

There was no way that Kerry could have prepared himself for what happened. At 4:30, in the Creative Visions Human Development Center, with a crush of television cameras and reporters crowded around him, Kerry waited for Rassmann to appear. When Rassmann made his way through the tangle of people and television equipment, he walked up to Kerry, opened his arms to embrace him, and dissolved into sobs. The emotion in the room was overwhelming as Rassmann—a large, husky man—wept in Kerry's arms. Kerry cupped his hands around Rassmann's face. The two men looked at each other. Jaded reporters were moved to tears. Finally the two men spoke to the crush of interviewers.

The first question was obvious: why was Rassmann there? "I'm a news junkie," he said. "I've followed John's career since 1984. I wrote him a letter then and invited him to dinner if he ever came to L.A. Never heard back. I'm a Volvo Republican, a practical idealist. He stands for things I'd like to stand for. And he's an honest man. With a good healthy ego, but not an ego that knows no bounds."

Rassmann then described what had happened between the two men all those years ago. "John didn't have to, but he came to the front under fire," Rassmann said, stopping to correct himself. "The bow, pardon me, sir. I always had a problem with navy terminology. And pulled me over. Had he not, there's no question in my mind that I would've fallen back into the river. He could've been shot and killed at any time, and so could I." Rassmann stopped. "So I figure I probably owe this man my life."

Finally, Kerry spoke. "This," he said, "is a brave, unbelievably patriotic American."

"He's going to get my vote," Rassmann added, as if the obvious needed to be stated.

When the reunion was over, Rassmann left with Kerry. He would stay with him through Caucus Day. He had come to Iowa to lend Kerry a hand, but he had done much more than that. Starting that night and continuing into Sunday, every local television station ran footage of Rassmann embracing Kerry, Kerry clutching Rassmann's face in his hands, and Rassmann telling the reporters he owed his life to Kerry. The reunion had happened so quickly, and the event itself was so badly planned, that no reporter doubted its authenticity. So programmers did not hesitate running it as the lead story—all over the state.

On the day of the Kerry-Rassmann reunion, Howard Dean had made the mistake of having a question-and-answer session at an event during which an elderly man asked him about senior citizens' issues. What the television cameras caught was an exchange that ended when Dean, whom the man interrupted as he tried to qualify his question, erupted into a rage. Angry and red-faced, Dean screamed at the old man from the stage. Dean was featured on the evening news screaming at a senior citizen—right after the gut-wrenching lead story about the Kerry-Rassmann reunion.

"This man was asking Dean something about prescription drugs or health care," says Douglas Brinkley, who was in Iowa at the time. "So Dean started answering his question, and the guy said, 'Yeah, but I've heard that. That's not what I said, Governor. What I'm asking. . . .' And then Dean said, 'Look, you sit down and you be quiet. And you let me answer!' The contrast, for a state like Iowa, with a heavy senior population, was between Kerry being embraced by a man whose life he saved and Dean badmouthing a guy who did nothing more than maybe push his question a little hard. You know, it was—boom, there it was."

Rarely had political imagery been so important. The pictures of Kerry showed him as a gentle, loving father figure who had been an authentic hero, a life-saver, in Vietnam—*the real deal*, as his campaign said—while Dean was shown as volatile and hot-tempered—the "angry man" gone nuts. These two scenes, shown time and again on sets all across Iowa, did more than anything in the final hours of the campaign to help voters decide for whom they were going to caucus on Monday. For Kerry, the timing could not have been better. For Dean, it could not have been worse.

That Saturday night, there was more news—good for Kerry and bad for Dean—when *The Des Moines Register* released its last poll before the caucus. The polling had ended on Friday night, and the pollsters had spent Saturday analyzing the results, which suggested that as supporters left Dean they were flocking not to Gephardt, as would have been expected, but to Edwards and to Kerry. Dean had fallen to third. The numbers were Kerry 26, Edwards 23, Dean 20, and Gephardt 18. By Saturday night, with the Rassmann reunion behind him and the *Register* poll released, Kerry was ready to say privately, if not publicly, that he was going to win on Monday.

On Sunday, *The New York Times* finally crystallized what had been happening in Iowa for weeks and accelerating in the last few days: "Interviews with dozens of new Kerry supporters and still undecided voters this week suggest that many Iowans once enchanted by Howard Dean, but alienated by a steady diet of critical reports about him, have begun to swing Mr. Kerry's way. And Mr. Kerry . . . has been enjoying consistently favorable coverage for the first time." That coverage continued the next day, when Kerry and his daughters attended services at the Antioch Baptist Church in Waterloo where, at one point in the service, they hugged their neighbors as an offering of peace. That night, Kerry held a rally of 1,800 supporters—again there were hordes of veterans and firefighters—and Ted Kennedy attended to introduce him.

For his part, Dean was desperate to regain lost ground. Out of nowhere, the campaign decided at the last minute to introduce Judith Steinberg Dean to Iowa voters. She had never been to Iowa; she had never given a major television interview. She was a physician and a mother, and, even though her husband was running for president, she had publicly stated her intention not to campaign for him—and she had not. But now, with the Dean campaign in full panic mode in the hours left before the caucus on Monday, the campaign's walking symbol of "we have completely screwed this thing up" arrived at the airport. She asked the Deaniacs and the press who were there to call her Judy Dean.

She arrived on Sunday afternoon, on a Lear 35 from Burlington. She preferred to be called Dr. Steinberg when she was with patients or in at the hospital and Judy Dean when she was filling the role of wife or mother or candidate spouse, the latter of which she rarely did. She had almost never campaigned with Dean when he was running for governor in Vermont. Luckily for her, the job of first lady of Vermont had not been time-consuming, so she had never had to curtail her medical practice in any way. Dean had been campaigning in Iowa for two years now, and today—the day before Caucus Day—was the first she had set foot in the state. She was Dean's "Sunday surprise," as the scheme became known. It was the brainchild of Ruth Harkin, Tom Harkin's wife, who had certainly hit the trail for her husband over the years—that was for sure. Like many candidate spouses, Ruth Harkin wouldn't have had it any other way.

When Judy Dean landed at the Davenport airport, she waited on the plane for her husband, who himself had flown into the airport on a Gulfstream jet from Plains, Georgia. For reasons that would never be fully explained, Dean had boarded his Gulfstream early that morning and flown to Plains so he could attend church with former president Jimmy Carter and his wife, Rosalyn. After the church service, Carter met with reporters, as Dean stood at his side, and while he went out of his way to praise Dean, particularly the courage he had shown early on when he was willing to challenge Bush, Carter would not endorse him. He even praised the other Democratic candidates, again as Dean stood at his side. The message seemed to be that Dean was so bent on being photographed with Carter that he would fly to Plains and go to church with him even if Carter refused to endorse him. Needless to say, Dean's moment in the spotlight with Carter did not achieve its desired result.

Since his and Judy's jets arrived at about the same time, the campaign decided they would be photographed getting off a plane together, even though they had flown in separately. So, the reporters covering Dean were herded into the airport terminal, far enough away so that photographers and cameramen would not be able to shoot Judy getting off her plane alone. After staffers had escorted her onto Dean's plane, the press was then taken back onto the tarmac, where they were left to stand in windy, seven-degree weather for twenty minutes as the Deans prepared for their appearance. Finally, they stepped out of Dean's Gulfstream, waving to a nonexistent crowd, as if they had been traveling together.

They were both smiling, the happy candidate and the candidate's happy spouse. There was only one problem. No one had ever seen this woman before. Instead of making voters feel more comfortable with Dean, having been reassured that he actually did have a wife, her sudden materialization raised obvious questions: Where had she been? Why had she not been here before? One hour after their "tarmac arrival," when the couple appeared at a rally at nearby West High School, Judy Dean tried to explain away some of the mystery surrounding herself and "Howard," as she called him. "For those of you who might not know"—that would have been everyone in the audience at the moment—"my name is Judy Dean. I haven't been here with Howard as much as I would like. We have a son in high school, a daughter in college, and I have a medical practice in Vermont with patients that depend on me daily. I wanted to come here today, and I wanted to say thank you to Iowa, and to support my husband for president, Howard Dean."

Her comments raised more questions than they answered. Why would a son in high school and a daughter in college keep her tied to Vermont so completely that, for the entire two years Dean had campaigned in Iowa, she had not been able to travel here once? Yes, doctors have patients, but they also have colleagues who can be called on during vacations and other obligations that require them to travel. In all of these two years, had Judy Dean not been able to arrange for another doctor to cover her duties so that she could have come to

Iowa and campaign with her husband? Any voter could draw the obvious conclusion: she could have come sooner, but she didn't.

The message of Judy Dean's surprise arrival in Iowa was exactly the opposite of what she was trying to project to the public: it looked like Dean had trotted out his wife because his campaign was falling apart. There was the same air of desperation about her arrival that had surrounded Dean's strange trip to Plains to stand beside Jimmy Carter. Indeed, following a second rally on Sunday night, Judy Dean did not even spend the night with her husband but flew back to Vermont because, as the campaign explained, she had to see patients the next day. Never in the history of medicine had a doctor been in such demand that she would not spend Caucus Day with her husband when he was running for president.

The campaign never adequately dealt with the strangeness that Judy Dean's sudden arrival and equally sudden departure suggested to the voting public. Regardless, it was too late. Even before Judy Dean got to Iowa that Sunday, the fate of her husband's campaign had been sealed.

On the evening of Monday, January 19, Iowa held its caucuses at 1,993 locations across the state. In a caucus, voters show up at a designated location—an elementary school lunch room, a high school gym, a community center—and, when all of the caucus-goers have gathered, they raise their hands as each candidate's name is called. Unlike a primary, where a voter can arrive at any point during the day to cast a ballot in a voting booth, a caucus has more of a community feel. The voters are all packed into a room at the same time. A candidate must have the support of 15 percent of the voters at any given caucus location to qualify. If he does not qualify, his supporters must then vote for another candidate. A caucus can lead to unpredictable results, since caucus-goers can change their minds as they are watching other people vote.

John Kerry began Caucus Day by attending Catholic mass with his family and close staff; no press coverage was allowed. Then he made several stops to make sure his campaign was getting out the vote. His last stop was in Cedar Rapids, where he had the Real Deal Express show up unannounced at a caucus site that was preparing for the night's events. The site, a high school in a neighborhood consisting of voters who were mostly Independents and blue-collar Democrats, was busy with caucus-goers milling about, waiting for the event to begin. When Kerry walked through the school's entranceway, cheers rose up from the crowd. People seemed surprised that an actual candidate was appearing at a caucus site on Caucus Day.

Soon, a 40-year-old woman approached Kerry. "My seventy-nine-year-old mother is voting for the first time in her life," the woman said. "She's voting for you because you are willing to speak out for veterans. My father was a Korean War veteran who passed away." As an aide tugged on Kerry's arm for him to leave—he could not be present at a caucus site when the actual caucusing began or he would be in violation of party rules—Kerry pulled away and told the woman he needed to see her mother. He had to thank her for her support. The woman led him through the crush of people until they found her mother. Kerry reached down and hugged her. "I want to thank you for your vote," he said. Finally, the staff succeeded in pulling Kerry away from the caucus room, and Kerry and his aides left the high school.

On the bus, heading back for Des Moines, Kerry sat in a front seat and began to think about the campaign. With David Wade and Bob

Shrum beside him, he reminisced. "Remember when we were out here for the first time, two years ago?" Kerry said as the bus raced down the road. "Mount Pleasant. A three-man campaign team." In those early days, Kerry traveled the state in a car or a minivan; sometimes he used a puddlejumper that he piloted himself. He loved looking down onto the cornfields that stretched out below him as he flew. "I really did learn to measure where we were in the year by the height and color of the corn. It's been an incredible experience out here. We've been up, down, in between." He stopped. "As for tonight, who knows, man," he said, laughing. Then Kerry eased back in his seat, closed his eyes, placed his hands in his lap, and dozed off. These were the catnaps, he often told his staff, that he had learned to take in Vietnam.

As Kerry slept, a voice rose up from the back of the bus. "David Wade! Come back here." It was David Halbfinger of *The New York Times*. Wade started back, but Halbfinger met him halfway. He whispered to Wade that, based on the earliest exit polls, Fox News was reporting that Kerry was winning. He was beating Dean by two points. "Take nothing for granted," Wade said. It had become the mantra for the campaign.

When Kerry woke up, the lights of Des Moines stretched out before him. Soon the bus arrived at the Hotel Fort Des Moines, and Kerry rushed upstairs to the presidential suite on the tenth floor. Before long, his staff was telling him that, based on the numbers they were seeing at headquarters, it looked like he might actually win. "I'd rather not think about it until we know something for sure," he said. "Maybe I'm too superstitious, but I am what I am."

Kerry had everyone leave except Gene Thorson, a native of Ames, Iowa, who had served on swift boat 94 with Kerry on the Mekong Delta in early 1969. Kerry and Thorson talked by themselves until they were joined by Teresa, who had spent the day campaigning in three important cities—Mason City, Sioux City, and Council Bluffs. Teresa first got word that Kerry might win when, arriving at the hotel from the airport, she was stopped downstairs by Carl Cameron of Fox News.

"Congratulations," Cameron had said.

Teresa stopped and looked at him. "Congratulations?" she said. "For what?"

"The exit polls," Cameron said. "Kerry is ahead."

"He is?" Teresa said. "Well, thank you for saying so."

Upstairs, when Kerry and Teresa first saw each other, they were overjoyed. Only 41 days ago, the day Al Gore had endorsed Howard Dean in Harlem, it had looked like Kerry was finished; now he might win.

Later, after Thorson left, Kerry and Teresa had dinner alone in the suite. Soon, Kerry's daughters, Alexandra and Vanessa, arrived, as did Kerry's brother, Cam, and his sisters, Peggy and Diana. Eventually, Thorson returned with other veterans, including Jim Rassmann. One person not in the suite was Max Cleland, whom the campaign had sent that day to the northern part of the state. "On election night," Cleland says, "as we were driving back in the dark, the returns started coming in, and I realized that Kerry was going to win Iowa. I told the people in the car, I said: 'The earth has just moved.' "

Back in the hotel suite, the phone rang constantly as it began to appear that Kerry would not only win, but take the contest by a large margin, with Edwards—not Dean—coming in second. Dean was polling a distant third, Gephardt fourth. It looked like Kerry had to get ready for a victory speech, so he went into the bathroom to shave. It was now that Mary Beth Cahill called from headquarters to tell Kerry that she had the official numbers: he had won.

Teresa said she would tell Kerry right away. She walked into the bathroom. "You won," she told Kerry as he stood at the counter and stared into the mirror, shaving cream all over his face. "You won."

Soon Kerry, in a dark business suit, joined what was now becoming a small mob of family and friends in the living room of the suite. As person after person hugged him, he drank a beer. The phone continued to ring. One call was from Howard Dean, who congratulated Kerry. The two spoke briefly. After some time, the suite's front door swung open and Max Cleland arrived in his wheelchair. Wearing a red plaid flannel shirt and blue jeans, he had spent the day campaigning in Marshalltown, which had the state's largest veterans' home. As an assistant pushed Cleland in, the room suddenly got quiet. Slowly, Kerry made his way through the crowded room. When he reached Cleland, he leaned down and hugged him. They held each other for a long time. "Max," Kerry said, "this is for you, my brother. We're getting the chance to finish the thing we started thirty years ago. For all of them."

In the elevator ride down to the ballroom, Kerry pulled out from his pocket a lucky four-leaf clover that an elderly woman had given him two days before when he was visiting a farm. The clover was wrapped in cellophane. "We need to find her," Kerry said. "I have to thank her. I'm going to ask her to call us." At the end of his speech, he did thank the woman, looking straight into the camera as he spoke.

The final margin of victory for Kerry was going to be greater than anyone had expected. The totals would be: Kerry 38 percent, Edwards 32, Dean 18, and Gephardt 11. The overflow crowd in the hotel ballroom exploded into a huge ovation when Kerry entered accompanied by his family and friends. Before Kerry started to speak, he noticed that Cleland was not on the stage, which did not have a wheelchair ramp. Four firefighters lifted Cleland up onto the stage in his wheelchair, so Kerry could begin.

He started off with the obvious. "Not so long ago," he said, "this campaign was written off. Thank you, Iowa, for making me the comeback Kerry!" It was a reference to the famous speech that Bill Clinton had given when, upon finishing second in the New Hampshire primary in 1992 after the Gennifer Flowers scandal had almost destroyed his campaign, he declared himself the "Comeback Kid."

After the cheering died down, Kerry continued. "If I am elected president," he began before he was stopped by the crowd, who shouted, "When! When! When!"

"*When* I am elected president," Kerry corrected himself. "I'm still learning!"

Then, in the middle of what ended up being a twenty-eight-minute speech, even though he had only three pages of prepared remarks, Kerry delivered a passage that *The New York Times* would describe as "the most concise and cutting indictment of Mr. Bush the famously wordy Mr. Kerry has ever given": "This President has an open hand for his friends at Halliburton, but he has turned his back on our friends and neighbors. He has turned his back on America's teachers and America's schools. And I will crisscross this country in this campaign and hold George W. Bush accountable for making a mockery of the words 'no child left behind.'"

Whether or not that was Kerry's best assault of the many he launched at Bush throughout the campaign, the speech did showcase Kerry to a national television audience, who had tuned in to see a victory speech by the media's darling, Howard Dean, only to find instead this statesmanlike, well-spoken senator from the East—someone who looked like a president.

When the speech was over, after the cheering had stopped and the cries of "Bring it on!" had died down, Kerry did a series of television interviews. The last one was with Joe Battenfeld of the local Fox affiliate in Boston. "Senator, you've won Iowa, but you're still far down in New Hampshire," Battenfeld said. "If you lose New Hampshire, do you really think . . ." But Kerry cut him off. "Joe, don't even go there." Kerry was smiling. "I won Iowa. I intend to win New Hampshire. I intend to be the nominee, and I'm going to beat George Bush, period. You'll see that soon. I'm going to keep working until I do because there are a lot of good people counting on me to do it."

Earlier in the evening, Howard Dean delivered what he had hoped was going to be his victory speech. As it turned out, he had done worse in the caucus than any pundit had predicted—so much so that he was not even sure how to explain it to the crowd that had assembled. He wanted to send a message to the Deaniacs across the country: don't be disheartened by the Iowa results. There would be many states in which he could still win. So, when Dean arrived on stage, accompanied by Tom and Ruth Harkin, his strongest supporters in Iowa, he believed that he had to show his fans—in the hotel ballroom and watching on television—unbridled optimism.

As the crowd cheered, Dean took off his coat. In the wall of people behind him on stage, Harkin loomed prominently. He was clapping like everyone else. Then Dean started his speech. Some of the lines sounded odd. "I'll see you around the corner, around the block," he said about his rivals. At another point, he shouted: "We will not give up. We will not quit, now or ever. We have just begun to fight! We have just begun to fight!" Finally, disaster. "We're going," he said, his emotions building, "to South Carolina and Oklahoma and Arizona and North Dakota and New Mexico. We're going to California and Texas and New York!" He added even more states before ending with Washington. Then he did it. "Aggggggggggggrrrrrrrrr!" he growled, swinging his clenched fist in front of him as his eyes alternately bugged and squinted. "Hahahahahahahahaha!" He may have been laughing, but he looked furious or, even worse, unhinged. He may have fired up the 3,500 people in the ballroom, but for all of the millions watching at home on national television, it was a bizarre performance. He did not appear to be a man stable enough to be president.

When the results of the Iowa caucus started coming in, it had become apparent that Dean was going to track at the level some political observers expected him to when he had first gotten into the race two years earlier—that of a fringe candidate who would place third or fourth in each primary or caucus he entered. But because of the relentless media hype he had generated in the summer, his showing in Iowa was a catastrophe. Then came the scream. Simply put, Howard Dean may have been able to overcome his bad showing in Iowa, given the national media's willingness to show him in a positive light no matter what he did, but he could not live down the scream. It was so strange, so unsettling, that it became an ongoing news story. Not since Edmund Muskie cried while standing in a snowstorm in New Hampshire in the 1968 race had one moment so captivated the public and completely devastated a presidential campaign.

"Howard Dean," as Roger Stone puts it, "might have survived

the defeat without the howl, and he might have survived the howl without the defeat, but the combination of the two was too devastating. That was the turning point. The scream didn't look presidential. Television is a very cool medium. My guess is, for the people in the room, they probably liked it. But on television he came across as a guy who was out of control. And you never want the President of the United States to look like he's out of control. Ever. That was Dean's fatal mistake."

For some, the irony was apparent. "The buzz from the Dean side," says Christopher Heinz, who spent the last week campaigning across the state with actor Scott Wolf and musicians Max Weinberg and Tom Delong of Blink 182, "was that they had this vaunted organization that was going to make everything happen. It just didn't happen. There was no perfect storm. It was a beautiful day that day, a clear day in Iowa."

Besides Kerry, the real surprise in Iowa was John Edwards, the first-term North Carolina senator who had stunned the political world by finishing not only second but a strong second. "On January 4," says Jennifer Palmieri, the communications director for Edwards, "John Edwards gave what James Carville called 'the greatest stump speech'—the 'two Americas' speech—and that's the speech he kept using all the way through to the end. On Saturday night, we found out we were second in *The Des Moines Register* poll, and then on Sunday we got the endorsement of the *Register*. On Caucus Night, we discovered Gephardt was in much worse shape all along than anybody realized and Dean was—just possibly—never for real. Back in the fall, people had the luxury of being able to flirt with Dean and be infatuated with the rebel and the troublemaker because they knew the caucuses were months away. People got serious when they needed to. The Iowa caucuses worked. They ferreted out the two best candidates, Kerry and Edwards."

In the end, even Edwards's impressive showing could not upstage Kerry, who since early November had lived through what *The Boston Globe* would call "one of the most spectacular turnarounds in modern American politics." He won because he had the boldness to make a change in his campaign when he had to, an action some candidates might not have taken. He won because, once he had made that staff change, he became a better candidate, a transition he achieved because he listened to what voters were telling him. He won because he had around him a core group of friends and family who would not let him commit a fatal mistake; blunders, maybe, but never a fatal mistake. At the center of Kerry's inner circle was Teresa Heinz Kerry, the person who ended up being a favorite of Iowa voters precisely because she always said what was on her mind. "If Kerry had a secret weapon in Iowa," one insider says, "it was Teresa. The people of Iowa simply fell in love with her, her candidness, her openness. She would hold meetings and people didn't want her to leave. Since they've been married, it's impossible to overestimate the role Teresa has played in John Kerry's life, both political and personal." It would also be hard to overestimate the role she played in his victory in Iowa.

"My mom loved Iowa," Christopher Heinz says. "People want to talk issues out there, and my mom loves to talk about issues. So many people came up to me and said, 'You know, I liked your stepdad. I wasn't sure. But then I saw your mom, and I'm definitely caucusing for John after meeting your mom.' That happened to me at probably every stop I made in Iowa. My mom communicates well, and she had a story to tell about America that I think really connects with people—you know, about being first-generation American and about growing up in a dictatorship."

The people in Iowa," Teresa Heinz Kerry says, "they are close to the earth. They don't deal in esoteric things, you know? They just have to deal in making things grow, making sure they do. Making ends meet, and living simply. They are very creative people." Teresa Heinz came to know Iowans because she spent so much time there—thirty-six days on thirteen different trips over five months. Most of the campaigning brought her into direct contact with voters. She held meetings in restaurants, cafés, homes. "There is a feeling of wanting to hope again, of wanting to have one's head up again," she says about what she learned from the people she met. "Not out of bravado, but out of dignity and honor and self-respect and hope—just hope—in the future." But mostly Teresa Heinz felt connected with Iowans because of the landscape. "Where I grew up in Africa," she says, "it was savannah, so it's not luxurious like the forest. I was in parts of Iowa, northern Iowa, in the middle center, bordering on Minnesota, where it's all farming, and when you drive you can see ahead of you there, a little cluster. Some trees, some silos, some little houses, and it looks just like a little dorp in Africa. Iowa is flat and open. You can see everywhere. Stand on a little place and you can see north, south, you name it."

In that flat landscape that reminded her of her early home in Africa, she might have been Kerry's best proponent. " 'John is this, John is that,' they say—'aloof' being the one that they started out with most," she says. "Anyway, names. And I think what happens when people meet me is, they see that I'm real, and that I truly am interested in issues. It's not just a job or something. I'm interested in it, and therefore it becomes relevant. And they say: 'If this guy is married to somebody like that, and she is really, truly interested and passionate about these things, and thinks about them in complex ways, there's a side to him we don't know.' I give a different flavor to John. That's how I'm his secret weapon."

6

THE SECRET
WEAPON

I think I must have been a tree in another life," Teresa Heinz said
to a reporter one afternoon in October of 2001 as she sat in the
living room of the townhouse on Beacon Hill that she and Kerry
bought after they were married in 1995. They chose the house for its
size—six stories (including the basement)—and she and Kerry decorated it together, selecting classic pieces of furniture to give the place
a warm, preppy feel with a bit of a European flair. There were afghans
and red leather sofas and armchairs and walls of books and portraits
of family members, a piece of modern art here, there an environment-
friendly handwoven tapestry. "I lived in trees when I was a child." She
was talking about a youth spent in southern Africa. "I'd also be at my
piano every day from the time I was five, or reading books. We didn't
have television. So we played. Nature taught me lessons. I think nature is the best teacher."

When Teresa Heinz talks about her early years in the Portuguese
colony of Mozambique, it sounds like a life out of an Isak Dinesen

novel. "My heart cries for Africa in a sense selfishly," she said. "The smell of Africa. But my memory bank is finite and I can't reconstruct it." Her father, Jose Simoes-Ferreira, was an oncologist, and her mother, Irene Thierstein, came from a wealthy British family, so Teresa grew up in affluence. The middle of three children, she started boarding school at age 12 in South Africa, where she organized student protests against apartheid. Her father wanted her to be a doctor, but she resisted. "Daddy, I want to be married and have kids," she told him. At the University of Witwatersrand in Johannesburg, she studied romance languages and literature. Graduating in 1959, she entered the Interpreters School of the University of Geneva. She would master five languages.

In Geneva, she met a handsome young man named John Heinz— he was called Jack—who was working at a Swiss bank before entering the family business back in Pittsburgh, the H. J. Heinz Food Company. Jack and Teresa met on a tennis court, then ran into each other at social functions, but when he returned to America, they didn't see each other for fourteen months. In 1964, Teresa took a job as an interpreter in Washington at the Department of State, and she and Jack started dating. Soon, she moved to New York City to work as a language consultant at the United Nations, where she remained until she and Jack were married in the Heinz Chapel in Pittsburgh on February 5, 1966.

While Jack, whom close friends called Pickles because of the family business, worked at the company headquarters in Pittsburgh, the couple had their first son, John IV, in 1967, and their second, Andre, in 1969. In 1971, when a seat in the House of Representatives in Pennsylvania came open, Heinz decided to run. Heinz was a moderate "Rockefeller Republican," which boded well for him in a bellwether state like Pennsylvania. At one campaign stop, Heinz was late, so Teresa took his place. "I got up there and started to talk about democracy and human rights and what it was like to live in South Africa," she says. "I talked for forty-five minutes. When Jack finally walked through the door with a big smile on his face, hobbling on crutches—he had broken his leg skiing before the campaign started—his campaign manager said, 'You don't need to come. She's done it already.' "

Teresa continued to campaign for Heinz—one of the first times a candidate's wife had been used as a surrogate so often—and he won. That year, Teresa became a U.S. citizen. The Heinzes' youngest son, Christopher, was born in 1973. Then, in 1976, Heinz ran for the Senate and won. "This time, I campaigned for him six out of seven days a week," Teresa says. "I had one day off." Reelected in 1982 and 1988, Heinz was said to be considering a run for the presidential nomination. Then, on the afternoon of April 4, 1991, not far from the Philadelphia International Airport, a small chartered plane carrying Heinz collided in midair with a helicopter. Heinz was killed, along with five other people. He and Teresa had just celebrated their twenty-fifth wedding anniversary.

In the wake of her husband's death, Teresa was devastated but unable to take the private time that she needed to grieve. She had inherited the responsibility for one of America's largest fortunes, which consisted of Heinz's personal holdings but also several heavily endowed family foundations. Teresa was being pressured by Republican Party leaders to take her husband's Senate seat. She refused to be appointed by the governor to fill his unfinished term, opting to devote her time to philanthropy—by heading the Howard Heinz Endowment and the Heinz Family Philanthropies—and to her three sons, the youngest of whom, Christopher, was 18 when his father died. Two years later, Teresa refused to run in the regular election. At a press conference in February of 1993, she attacked the political establishment by saying, "The best ideas for change unfortunately no longer come from political campaigns. Today, political campaigns are the graveyard of real ideas, and the birthplace of empty promises."

Teresa later softened, although she never got over her first husband's death. In fact, for years after she married Kerry, when Teresa referred to "my husband" she meant John Heinz. She routinely referred to Kerry, even in the early months of their marriage, as "John Kerry." When the idiosyncracies of how she referred to the two men became the subject of press reports, she felt the need to clarify what she meant. "I've had two husbands," she told the reporter that day in October of 2001 in the living room of her townhouse, "and the other one was a longer husband. This"—John Kerry—"is my *now* husband. That"—John Heinz—"was my *then* husband. The then husband is the father of my kids, the grandfather of my grandchild. He taught me to be a woman. He was the man of my life. What can I say? Now I'm lucky that I have another husband. Very serious, interested in things, and there's a lot of compatibility. But I can't compare the two. This is another chapter."

Yes, the environment did it," Kerry said, referring to what he and his wife say brought them together.

Kerry had joined Teresa in the living room of their Boston brownstone. In Washington, they lived in the white stucco Georgetown mansion—once the home of a czarist Russian ambassador—where Teresa and her late husband raised their three sons. She also owned a 100-acre estate, Rosemont Farm, in the Pittsburgh suburb of Fox Chapel, where she and Heinz lived when they were not in Washington. She owned a ski lodge in Sun Valley, Idaho, and an oceanfront mansion in Nantucket as well. Today, they sat beside each other in red leather chairs.

"The environment," Teresa concurred, her speech colored by a faint European accent. "We always kept meeting around the environment."

In the late 1980s, Kerry and Teresa Heinz had seen each other in passing, since Kerry and John Heinz served together in the Senate. John Heinz introduced Teresa to Kerry on Earth Day in 1990, when both men spoke on the steps of the Capitol. But the first meaningful encounter between Kerry and Teresa occurred after John Heinz's death, when they met in 1992 at the United Nations Earth Day Summit in Rio de Janeiro. Kerry had gone as a member of the Senate delegation, Teresa as a delegate appointed by President George H.W. Bush.

"We happened to meet there," Kerry said, "and several of us went out to this outrageously funny dinner. Frank Lautenberg, Larry Pressler, myself, Teresa. The next day, we went to church together with a small group, and I have maintained to this day that it was my singing in Portuguese . . ."

"No!" Teresa interrupted in jest. "It was Larry Pressler who sang in Portuguese."

"I know it was," Kerry said, conceding the point.

At the summit, Teresa was listening to a speech in Portuguese when she suspected that the interpreter was misinterpreting on purpose, so she stopped the speech, made the interpreter sit down, and began translating the speech herself—a move that impressed Kerry because it showed that Heinz could be aggressive and forthright.

"Anyway," Kerry said, "we came back. Then another environmental thing brought us together. The Japanese minister of the environment was there, and we went out to dinner."

"He wasn't a minister then," Heinz said.

"He was going to *become* a minister, correct," Kerry said, "and we all went out to dinner with him in Washington."

That dinner was in February of 1994. Following the meal, the couple ended up taking a midnight stroll that took them to the Vietnam Memorial on the Washington Mall. After that night, they started dating. Soon Teresa discovered that, for Kerry, Vietnam was a subject that was never too far away. Even in his sleep, Kerry was haunted by Vietnam in nightmares.

"The first nightmare I heard, I was actually not with him," Teresa said. "Before we got married, I was sleeping with one of his daughters in this little shed, a little barn it was. And the wall was just wood. And he was in this little captain's room, and, you know, I was asleep and Alexandra, his daughter, was there. Then, all of a sudden, the walls were coming down in the house. I said, 'Oh!' And Alex said, 'It's just Dad.' "

Kerry laughed uneasily.

"So I went back to bed," Heinz continued, "and he hit the walls again and I nearly died. I said, 'Holy mackerel!' The next morning, I said, 'What did you dream about?' He said, 'Why?' I said, 'Because you broke down the house almost.' He said, 'Vietnam.' "

Kerry looked over at Teresa. "I'm amazed you ever came back," Kerry said, laughing.

"I wanted to see it for real," Heinz said without missing a beat.

In December of 1994, they were engaged. *Forbes* once placed Teresa's personal fortune at $860 million; she also headed the billion-dollar Heinz family foundations, making her such a prominent force in the country's philanthropic community that *W* magazine dubbed her "Saint Teresa." When Kerry and Teresa married in a Catholic ceremony—Teresa was a devout Catholic like Kerry—on her Nantucket estate in May of 1995 before an audience of 100 guests, it was the ultimate merging of power and money—and, ironically, of two political parties. Kerry was a Democrat, Heinz a Republican. As Kerry liked to put it for years, "If you want bipartisanship, this is quintessential bipartisanship."

Once they were married and Teresa could see the nightmares for real, she discovered that Kerry was reliving his tours as a swift boat commander on the Mekong Delta. These days, Teresa said, Kerry had almost no nightmares—a product, perhaps, of his newfound contentment. "I think I really am a better human being," said Kerry, who in 1997 got a church annulment of his first marriage, "and I certainly am a much more relaxed person through the relationship that Teresa and I have than I was before. Still, it was a transition for both of us. It was a transition for Teresa out of mourning—out of years and years of a happy, wonderful marriage, out of the shock and loss of what happened to her suddenly—and so the realization that life goes on and you can find somebody. For me, it was a transition into a place of trusting somebody and believing you can have a full relationship and it doesn't betray you or burn you or leave you kind of confused."

On a clear, crisp evening in early November of 2001 in New York City, the elite of America's environmental movement were gathering at the Waldorf-Astoria Hotel for a dinner held annually by the League of Conservation Voters. Among the sold-out audience were political movers and shakers such as William Weld, Bill Richardson, Andrew Cuomo, John Podesta, Congressman Sherwood Boehlert, Lawrence Rockefeller, and Teddy Roosevelt IV. There were business and media heavyweights like Michael Oppenheimer and Charlie Rose. There was even Hollywood royalty in the person of Robert Redford. But in this roomful of boldface names, John Kerry and Teresa Heinz commanded the most attention.

Soon Kerry and Teresa took their places at the center table. He was the guest of honor, she a co-chair. Redford gave a glowing introduction, and Kerry took the podium.

The speech that followed was vintage Kerry: strongly worded, well delivered, unapologetically critical of Bush. "I believe," Kerry said that night, "it is a false patriotism that tries to suggest to us that—as a matter of national security, for energy independence and economic growth, as a response to September 11th—we should drill in the pristine wilderness of the Arctic National Wildlife Refuge." The audience erupted into applause. ANWR was one of the League's hot-button issues, and, like Kerry, they believed that the Bush Administration was trying to use the events of September 11th as an excuse to open up federally protected land in Alaska to oil drilling.

But Kerry was not finished criticizing Bush. "It is false patriotism," he continued, "that suggests that when four hundred and fifteen thousand of our fellow citizens lose their jobs in one month, our response should be to reward some of the wealthiest, most heavily sub-sidized oil and gas companies in America with more than twenty billion dollars in new tax giveaways."

It was an attention-grabbing speech clearly meant to capture the next day's headlines, which it did. In that way, Kerry was already running for president, even though he had not yet won reelection yet to the Senate. That happened in November of 2002, when he won his fourth term in a race where the Republicans did not put up a candidate against him. They had run the best in the state in

1996, William Weld, and Kerry had won handily, despite being down in the polls on Labor Day. In 2002, the Republicans didn't even bother.

In early 2003, Teresa Heinz changed her voter registration from Republican to Democrat. Despite the talk of "quintessential bipartisanship," when it was apparent that Kerry was running for president, his advisers determined that, to make sure Kerry could hold the Democratic base, Teresa needed to switch parties. At the same time, she also changed her name, at least for the purposes of the campaign. Until early 2003, Teresa had only used the last name Heinz, even within the context of Kerry's political career, but now Kerry advisers decided that she needed to become Teresa Heinz Kerry for recognition value. Even so, when a *Los Angeles Times* reporter asked her about the decision to change the name, she said, "No decision. My official name is still Teresa Heinz." She used "Kerry" when campaigning for her husband. If, for example, she was asked to give an autograph at a Kerry event, she signed, "Teresa Heinz Kerry."

Some aspects of her life did not change. Kerry might have been running for president, but Heinz remained outspoken. If there was one trait that came to be identified with her, in fact, it was her willingness to speak candidly and honestly at all times, even if what she had to say might offend people or sound unpolitical. Talking to an audience in Phoenix once, she addressed her right-wing critics, not for their politics but for the way they viewed her. "They"—conservative talk radio hosts like Rush Limbaugh and Sean Hannity, she meant—"don't like this shawl," she said, indicating one of the many different shawls she was known to wear draped over one shoulder or around her neck, "because it looks ethnic. I have news for them: I am ethnic. I'm Latin."

As the campaign unfolded, Heinz's involvement was not without its problems. In the press much was made out of the fact that she refused to release her tax returns. She refused to do this, she said, because her finances were commingled with those of her three sons, who were not public figures in the same way she was. Finally, she released a description of her tax returns for the year 2002, which showed that her personal income amounted to some $5 million on which she paid a more or less standard rate of income tax.

Heinz had always made it clear that, no matter what happened to Kerry, she would continue to head the Heinz philanthropies. So, while the campaign proceeded, a process she found enjoyable—"it's been wonderful," she says, "physically exhausting but not mentally exhausting at all, since I get very stimulated by discussions with people"—one obvious overriding question began to emerge; Given all of the roles she fills in her life—mother, stepmother, wife, businesswoman, community leader—did she want to be first lady? "It would be obviously an awesome, honorable thing to be," she says. "But it could also be a lot of fun in the sense of talking to people and exchanging ideas about how to go about getting our country in shape by enabling people to find their own solutions. I will, however, still keep my connections with my foundations. I will always make time for that."

7

NEW HAMPSHIRE

After the victory celebration in Des Moines on Caucus Day, John Kerry and his campaign headed straight for New Hampshire. They didn't even spend the night in Iowa; there was only one week until the New Hampshire primary. So, after Kerry did his last television interview, the campaign and the traveling press corps packed up to leave. One fact was hard to ignore: the press corps had grown. On Caucus Day on the Real Deal Express, Kerry had had eight reporters covering him. As Kerry started for the airport, he had fifty.

An emerging development in the campaign now became even more obvious. From the beginning, Kerry had had an antagonistic relationship with the national press corps assigned to cover him. On his announcement tour in September, reporters, some of whom were not subtle in their admiration of Dean, were openly hostile toward Kerry and his staff. This generally negative feeling was also reflected in the way the press covered Kerry and his campaign. Positive details of events went unreported, while any mistake Kerry or a staffer made was blown out of proportion. The overall dislike the press corps felt for Kerry was magnified by their numbers. With fifty of them on the plane—and the press corps would remain that size or get even larger—it was hard to miss their attitude.

"On the night of the Iowa caucus, we loaded our vans," says Christine Anderson, a campaign aide, "and the press and everyone headed for the airport. We went through the magnetometers and got on the plane, and everyone was barely awake. When we got on"—it was now 3 A.M.—"most people slept the entire ride back. We were awakened in the morning as they were serving breakfast on the plane. We started to get ready for a 7 A.M. rally in an airport hangar in Manchester." When Kerry got off the plane, he was greeted on the tarmac by Del Sandusky, one of the "crewmates," as they were now simply called, and Jeanne Shaheen. "We gotta win here," Kerry said to them. "We've got a week to do it. Lock and load."

The rally, held just after daybreak on Tuesday, marked the beginning of a whirlwind week of campaigning for the Kerrys. When they were not holed up in their suite at the Tage Inn in Manchester planning their next moves, they were traveling from one end of the state to the other. Kerry and Teresa kept separate schedules, and the surrogates were out in full force—Christopher Heinz, Alexandra and Vanessa Kerry, Max Cleland and the veterans (especially the crewmates), and Jeanne Shaheen. Only weeks before, some public-opinion polls had Kerry trailing in New Hampshire by thirty points. But all of that had changed, thanks to Iowa. Now the campaign would see if Mary Beth Cahill's slingshot strategy was going to work.

On Tuesday, there were developments in the other campaigns as well. The brain trust of the Dean campaign made a decision to end the Perfect Storm. As it turned out, Iowans were put off by the concept. The last thing that the average Iowan wanted was some out-of-state Gen-Y student type in a DEAN FOR AMERICA sweatshirt to come knocking on his door and tell him how to vote. The Dean campaign was afraid that New Hampshire voters, every bit as independent-minded as those in Iowa, would be similarly put off, so the Perfect Storm was ended. The campaign issued a press release saying that it would use people who actually lived in New Hampshire to tell other New Hampshirites why they should vote for Dean.

Halfway across the country in St. Louis, Dick Gephardt announced that, as a consequence of his poor showing in Iowa, he was dropping out of the presidential race and, in effect, retiring from public life, since he had decided some time back that he would not stand for reelection in his Congressional district. "I accept the results with the knowledge that I gave this campaign everything that I had in me," Gephardt said, his voice full of emotion. "My pursuit of the presidency has reached its end. I'm withdrawing as a candidate and returning to private life after a long time in the warm light of public service."

Tuesday night saw another consequence of the Iowa caucus, of sorts, when President Bush delivered the State of the Union Address to a joint session of Congress. Traditionally, the president gives this address in mid-January, but this year the White House decided to schedule the speech the day following the Iowa caucus, no doubt as a way to interfere with the attention the Democrats would be receiving. So, before a prime-time television audience on Tuesday night, Bush delivered the address—a not-so-subtle pitch for reelection. "We have not come all this way through tragedy and trial and war only to falter and leave our work unfinished," he said. "Americans are rising to the tasks of history, and they expect the same of us." Of Bush's four State of the Union addresses to date, this one, pundits observed, was

the least inspired. The speech coursed through a wide variety of topics and was on occasion weighted down with trivialities, such as when
Bush implored professional sports organizations to do something
about athletes using steroids. Not since Eisenhower had a president
given such a lackluster State of the Union Address presented in such
a mediocre manner. At the end of the night, Republican Party insiders
were horrified. Kerry's twenty-eight-minute victory speech the night
before, most of it delivered off the cuff, was a far better example of
oratorical skills.

With new enthusiasm, Kerry spent all of Wednesday on the campaign trail. At a rally in Nashua, he took direct aim at Bush and the
speech he had given the night before. "You can tell from his State of
the Union Address that the president is facing reelection," Kerry said.
"I wish he'd face reality. Watching President Bush's speech last night,
one thing kept coming back to me: he just doesn't get it." That night,
1,000 people showed up to hear Kerry at the Phillips Exeter Acad-
emy. It was his largest crowd in the state so far—and a clear indication that the slingshot strategy was working. But Kerry wasn't taking
any chances. He continued to say that he would fight for "every single vote" in New Hampshire, no matter what the opinion polls and
pundits said.

By Thursday, with Kerry's momentum building, the Dean campaign went into damage-control mode. With the polls suggesting
that Dean's support in New Hampshire was collapsing, the campaign
decided he needed to do something—anything—to counteract what
commentators and comedians were now referring to as his "I Have
a Scream" speech. So the campaign arranged for Dean and his wife
to be interviewed by Diane Sawyer on *Primetime Live*. The interview
would be taped in the afternoon and then aired that night after a televised debate, the last one before the primary on Tuesday.

Dean would need all the help he could get. On Thursday, all three major newspapers in Boston, a key media market for New Hampshire since many people in the area worked in Boston but lived—and voted—in New Hampshire, endorsed John Kerry. The *Boston Herald* declared: "John Kerry as a presidential candidate remains a work in progress [but] as a solid, thoughtful political leader [he] is a well-known commodity around these parts." *The Boston Phoenix* said: "In his private life, he served in Vietnam, where he was three times wounded and twice decorated for bravery. Recognizing the magnitude of our national error, he then helped lead the fight to change policy there, along the way helping to raise two daughters. He understands the balance between the public and the private. We think Kerry is the best of the field." *The Boston Globe* pronounced: "We share John Kerry's values and vision for America as a confident, tolerant, enlightened nation. By his consistency, his resolve, and his experience, he has continued to demonstrate that he is best prepared to help the nation realize those ideals." This was not faint praise from a newspaper that had often maintained an antagonistic relationship with the candidate.

On Thursday, Dean began his day with two town-hall meetings. Suffering from a runny nose, he was overcome at times with fits of coughing—the stress of the campaign no doubt showing in these symptoms. It was also obvious that the disaster of Iowa weighed heavily on his thinking. "Look, I'm not a perfect person," he told an audience in Lebanon. "I've got plenty of warts. I say things that get me in trouble. I wear suits that are cheap. But I say what I think, and I believe what I say, and I'm willing to say things that are not popular, but that ordinary people know are right. In other words, I lead with my heart and not with my head."

That afternoon, Dean and his wife taped their interview with

Sawyer. Then, it was on to the debate at the Dana Center Auditorium at St. Anselm College before an audience of 400 and moderated by Peter Jennings of ABC News. Kerry arrived at the debate led by a corps of bagpipe players from the firefighters' union; "just the sort of touch," *The New York Times* pointed out, "you might expect from a candidate riding a surge." These days the specifics of Kerry's public appearances were all routed through Cahill's office in Washington. Touches such as the bagpipe corps may have been suggested by local staffers planning and executing the events, but all decisions were ultimately made by Cahill. Once a schedule was put in place, a detailed daily memorandum was submitted in advance to Kerry, who had final say over which events he would do and the way those events would be executed.

During the debate that night, Kerry performed with confidence. The most controversial moment of the debate centered around Wesley Clark. At one point, Jennings confronted Clark about a comment that the filmmaker Michael Moore, a strong Clark supporter, had made the week before when he had called President Bush a "deserter." Clark stunned the audience by not debunking Moore's claim, saying instead that Moore had not been the only person to make such a charge. Clark's performance paralleled one he made on Monday night when, appearing on *Larry King Live,* he said, "I've won a war," meaning Kosovo. To this, former Republican senator and presidential candidate Robert Dole, also a guest on the show, quipped, "Politically, you just became a colonel instead of a general." This prompted Clark, for some reason, to respond to Dole by dismissing Kerry. "He's a lieutenant and I'm a general," Clark said. Obviously, things were not going well for the former NATO commander.

Naturally, one topic of the debate would be Dean's "I Have a Scream" speech. Dean tried to laugh off the speech as insignificant, which prompted Al Sharpton to say, "Don't be hard on yourself about hooting and hollering. If I had spent the money you did and got eighteen percent, I'd still be in Iowa hooting and hollering." Dean tried to appear unfazed by Sharpton's comment, but Sharpton was once again saying what many were thinking: it wasn't just that Dean had lost Iowa, but that he lost it badly. Here was a candidate about whom the media was already running stories speculating on his vice-presidential running mate, and he'd finished a distant third, twenty points behind the winner.

Dean's last best hope to do well in New Hampshire was the Diane Sawyer interview, which aired on ABC immediately after the debate. The interview had been taped in a common room of a local inn, with Sawyer sitting in a chair and Dean and Judy sitting across from her on a sofa. Sawyer had a television monitor ready so she could play clips of the "I Have a Scream" speech. Since Dean had seen the incident on tape only once, Sawyer played it for him while Judy watched. As the clip played, Dean seemed fascinated by his own behavior. "I was having a great time," he said to Sawyer. "Look at me!"

Sawyer asked the obvious question: Did the speech look unpresidential? Dean said quickly, "Well, I would certainly agree with that."

So Sawyer turned to Judy, who said that because she rarely watched television, she hadn't seen a replay of the speech until Wednesday. What did she think? Sawyer asked. "I thought it looked kind of silly," Judy said, her voice quiet and emotionless. "But I thought it looked okay."

Sawyer also brought up the issue of Judy's reluctant involvement in Dean's campaign. "I love Howard," said Judy, who wore a simple red sweater set, "and I think he would make a terrific president. And, I think if I can help him, I will. And that doesn't mean he's going to disrupt my life, disrupt my patients, my son, but if he calls on a Saturday, and I'm not on call that weekend, I'll be out there Sunday."

Dean himself chimed in on the issue of family. "I learned a long time ago," he said, "that all you have in your life is your family. My marriage and my family's the most important thing to me. More important than being president."

The point of the interview was to show Howard and Judy Dean in a favorable light so voters would view Dean as a quiet, well-mannered, thoughtful family man and doctor—not an explosive personality capable of lapsing into red-faced tirades. To this end, Dean stayed away from his "angry man" persona. In fact, not once on Thursday did he mention the war in Iraq, the issue that had brought him to national prominence in the first place. As evidence of their revised strategy, the Dean campaign began running a new ad in New Hampshire on Thursday. Entitled "Leader," it showed Jimmy Carter calling Dean "outspoken and courageous."

On Friday, Kerry attended a rally for veterans in Manchester. Along with the Veterans Brigade for Kerry, those veterans who were now constantly with him, Kerry was joined by Senator Ernest Hollings of South Carolina, who had endorsed him. In his remarks, Max Cleland said of Kerry: "The best thing we can call him is brother. Why? Because he's been there, done that, and gotten a few holes in his T-shirt." Hollings, also a veteran, was more blunt. "We're going to teach that fellow"—Wesley Clark—"in South Carolina that there are more lieutenants than there are generals, I can tell you that. John didn't give his life to another, but he was willing to, I can tell you that, time and time again." Later that day, Kerry got word that former Vice President Walter Mondale was ready to endorse him.

Then, as he was traveling to the day's last event, Kerry was given the latest poll figures for New Hampshire. The days when he was thirty points down were gone. He was now ahead. The slingshot strategy was working. A bumper sticker started showing up in New Hampshire that seemed to say it all. It read: DATED DEAN, MARRIED KERRY.

Earlier on Friday, Kerry added a new staffer to his campaign. After working for Richard Gephardt for twelve years, mostly in Congress but also on the campaign, Steve Elmendorf, whom the *Times* described as Gephardt's "political alter ego," was named Kerry's deputy campaign manager. While he had been especially close to Gephardt, Elmendorf was a good friend of Mary Beth Cahill, who hoped he would be helpful in bringing in support from members of Congress, labor, and the decision-makers in the gay and lesbian community, constituencies with whom Elmendorf had developed strong ties over the years.

Even as the race had unfolded in Iowa, rumors circulated in political and journalist circles that an "unholy alliance," to quote one observer, had been formed between the Kerry and Gephardt campaigns. It had one goal: to take out Dean at any cost. "Perhaps it was not so surprising," *The New York Times* reported in mid-October, "to see Representative Richard A. Gephardt and Senator John Kerry arm in arm, all smiles, whispering in each other's ears on stage at the Democratic debate Thursday night in Phoenix. These two presidential contenders, who for months have been eclipsed by the surging campaign of Howard Dean, have been fairly chummy of late—at Dr. Dean's expense." The newspaper then noted that at a debate in New York Kerry often went to the defense of Gephardt, and that "aides to both men . . . acknowledge that at least at the staff level, the Gephardt and Kerry campaigns are more than friendly; they are sharing information about Dr. Dean that helps fuel each other's attacks."

Late in 2003, a group was formed with the nebulous-sounding

title Americans for Jobs, Health Care, and Progressive Values. The group's president was a former Ohio Democratic congressman named Edward F. Feighan, who had contributed money to Gephardt's 2004 presidential campaign. Its treasurer was David Jones, a fund-raiser for Gephardt, and its spokesman was Robert Gibbs, who had worked for the Kerry campaign. Given the players who formed this political action committee, how could people in the know not speculate that something suspicious was in the works? Then the group's ads began to run.

The first ad revealed that Dean had received support from the National Rifle Association—a detail disturbing to hard-core Democrats since gun control had historically been a wedge issue for them. Two weeks later, the group aired an ad that would soon become notorious. As eerie music played, the screen was filled with a shot of Osama bin Laden on the cover of *Time*. Then, as the camera slowly zoomed in on his eyes, words popped up on the screen: DANGEROUS WORLD. DESTROY US. DANGERS AHEAD. NO EXPERIENCE. Finally, an ominous voice-over was heard: "Americans want a president who can face the dangers ahead. But Howard Dean has no military or foreign-policy experience. And Howard Dean just cannot compete with George Bush on foreign policy. It's time for Democrats to think about that— and think about it now."

The Dean campaign demanded to know who was funding Americans for Jobs, Health Care, and Progressive Values, but federal campaign finance laws did not require that information to be released for several months. "We will disclose donors when the law requires," David Jones said. Of course, the Kerry and Gephardt organizations denied any association with the group. Ultimately, disclosure forms would reveal that one of the group's largest backers was former New

Jersey senator Robert Torricelli, who had given the group $50,000 from monies left in his Senate reelection fund in 2002 when he dropped out five weeks before the election because of alleged unethical behavior. Torricelli had no official role in the Kerry campaign, but he had solicited money for Kerry and met with individuals who were raising money for Kerry.

"I don't care what people say," contends one Washington insider familiar with both the Kerry and Gephardt campaigns. "I believe Kerry and Gephardt teamed up to take out Dean." If so, it only made sense that Elmendorf would end up working for Kerry. But should the "unholy alliance" theory be true, it would prove a fact many people close to Kerry already knew: in politics, Kerry would do whatever it took, as long as it was ethical, to win.

On Saturday morning, Kerry played ice hockey with former members of the National Hockey League's Boston Bruins. When he was asked by a reporter after the game to comment on Michael Moore's depiction of Bush as a "deserter," Kerry called the language "over the top." Then, on Sunday, Kerry held rallies and appeared on *Fox News Sunday*.

Dean spent the weekend avoiding George Stephanopoulos, who had gone so far as to travel to New Hampshire, follow Dean around on Saturday, and rent a hotel room near where Dean was holding a campaign event on Sunday, on the off chance that Dean would appear on his show when he was done. Dean didn't. Nor did Dean appear on *Meet the Press*, even though Tim Russert had offered to give him the entire hour. Instead, Dean agreed to appear at a taping of *The Daily Show* with Jon Stewart for an interview that would run on

Comedy Central on Monday night. In the final hours before the New Hampshire primary, the campaign that the national media had once described as a juggernaut destined to carry its candidate to the nomination had, by ducking the Sunday morning network news shows in favor of a program to be aired on Comedy Central, literally become a joke.

On Sunday, Judy traveled with Dean, and together they did give four interviews, all with local television stations. One of them was with WMUR in Manchester. In that interview, Judy said: "I wanted to be here because I want to be with Howard, and he asked me to be here." The more the Dean campaign tried to fix its problem, the worse the problem became.

On Monday, Kerry spent the day going from one town-hall meeting to another. In Keene, he again announced that he would stay until the last question was answered. "I am not here just to count down the hours until tomorrow," he said, "or while them away, because we are fighting for every single vote in this state. And I have come here to mark with you the beginning of the end of the Bush presidency." Meanwhile, Dean spent the day campaigning with Judy, who canceled her meetings with patients for the day. After a successful rally in Manchester, Dean spoke briefly to a reporter from *The New York Times* about his campaign, its past and its future. "Once we got way out in front," he said, "our strategy was to try to blow open the race. And everybody else worked really hard in concert to make sure that didn't happen, and they succeeded. So now it's a long marathon. I think this is going to go a while, unless Kerry wins tomorrow, in which case there will really be a shakeout in a hurry."

The morning of the New Hampshire primary started out badly for Kerry. "It is five A.M.," says David Wade, who was sharing a room with Marvin Nicholson, Kerry's personal aide (the Tage Inn was short on rooms), "in our highway-side hotel that had become our week-long home, when Marvin and I are awakened from a dead sleep by a knock at the door: John Kerry is standing there in his towel. There is no hot water in his room, and he needed to shower for the round of morning shows. There was no hot water in our room either, so all three of us go up and down the hallway in search of a working shower, with none to be found. Finally, Kerry, still in a towel, showers as best he can while we microwave pans of hot water so he can shave and wash up before the shows." Somehow Kerry was out of his hotel room by 6:30 and ready to start the day.

After the morning shows, Kerry went to his state headquarters, lo-cated in an enormous, sprawling old mill building on the banks of the Merrimack River, where he spoke to an army of volunteers who would spend the day manning phone banks to get out the vote. "You never gave up on me," he said, "and I will never forget it. We were thirty points down and the temperature here was under zero, and you kept going. I'll never forget, and I'll never give up on you—ever. This state, this campaign, you're the most loyal people I could imag-ine in politics." Before Kerry left, Joey Duboise, a wheelchair-bound veteran, arrived at the headquarters. Kerry had told Duboise's story all over the country: how the government was denying him his dis-ability pay by deducting it from his pension. Duboise could barely afford the dialysis he required. The government seemed to want to make his life harder, not easier. Kerry went over to Duboise. "This is what it's all about, brother," Kerry said, reaching down to hug him.

All afternoon, Kerry was anxious. He was supposed to take time off and rest in his hotel room, but by the middle of the afternoon he was standing on a corner on Elm Street, the main drag that runs through Manchester, looking for hands to shake. As it turned out, he didn't need the extra push. That night, in a primary that saw a record turnout of some 218,000 voters, Kerry won by a 13-point margin. He received 39 percent of the vote, Dean 26, Edwards 12, Clark 12, and Lieberman 9. The race was so lopsided that the Associated Press declared Kerry the winner twenty-five minutes after the polls had closed. "New Hampshire was exciting," Peggy Kerry says, "considering that in the summertime John had been down 20, 30 points. But John had the sense, even in the summer, that he had traction in Iowa, and if that support held up he would do well not only in Iowa but in New Hampshire as well."

At the victory celebration, the mood was euphoric. "Thank you, New Hampshire," Kerry said when he took the stage, "for lifting up this campaign." He singled out the veterans who had worked so hard for him, many of whom were with him on the stage. "In the hardest moments of the past month," Kerry said, "I depended on the same band of brothers I depended on some thirty years ago. We're a little older, a little grayer, but we still know how to fight for our country." Kerry summed up the race: "I have only just begun to fight. I love New Hampshire, and I love Iowa, too. And I hope with your help to have the blessings and the opportunity to love a lot of other states in the days to come."

When Dean took the stage for his celebration, his mood was subdued, a deliberate counterpoint to the effects of the "I Have a Scream" speech. "Thank you—my goodness!" he said before a crowd that was considerably less excited than the one in Iowa. "The people of New Hampshire have allowed our campaign to regain its momentum, and I am very grateful. And the people of New Hampshire have allowed all of you to hope again that we are going to have real change in America."

that. But Dean did not understand that the Gore endorsement had probably hurt him more than it helped. Some voters viewed Gore as a loser; he may have won the popular vote in 2000, but he lost the election. Many Democrats simply didn't like him. Then there was the issue of his betrayal of Lieberman, a perception with the public that had gotten worse instead of better. Whatever the reason, the Gore endorsement was looking so much like a curse that one night on *Larry King Live!* Bob Dole joked: "My advice to Kerry and Edwards is, if Gore calls, don't take the call. I mean, it may be an endorsement."

On Wednesday night, Dean held a conference call with reporters to announce that Trippi had left the campaign and Neel was taking over as CEO. "Roy brings enormous experience both in management and national politics," Dean said. "I felt we've needed a strong organization force in the office."

As Dean's drama unfolded, Kerry campaigned in Missouri. He was in a good mood. Before his plane had left Boston, he spoke with reporters on the tarmac in the snow. Then, on the plane, he sat in his seat in the front row and played his guitar. When he finished, he tossed a football with an aide—not an easy feat to accomplish on a cramped airplane aisle.

Kerry arrived in St. Louis to receive the endorsements of former senator Thomas Eagleton; former senator Jean Carnahan, the widow of former governor Mel Carnahan; and Mayor Francis Slay of St. Louis. "You hear that thunderous applause?" Eagleton said to Kerry after Eagleton was introduced at a rally. "I'd make a hell of a vice president."

That was now one of Kerry's main concerns: who would he pick as his running mate? He had run in only two races—Iowa and New

Hampshire—but it looked like he had the momentum. While many journalists realized the mistake the media had made about Dean, few admitted it, especially in print. "The results . . . in New Hampshire," John Podhoretz wrote in the *New York Post*, "represent a humiliating disaster for the mainstream media. The political reporters and editors who have been judging this race for a year have made utter fools of themselves. Nobody foresaw John Kerry's huge victory in Iowa. . . . But there could be no more infamous an example of the political media's gullibility than the Zeppelin candidacy of Howard Dean. . . . The press has been wrong about everything. Everything. Keep that in mind for the rest of the year. You can be sure that the political media won't remind you of it."

8

SUPER TUESDAY

Before Super Tuesday, there would be other important dates—Little Super Tuesday, February 3, when seven states (Arizona, Delaware, Missouri, New Mexico, North Dakota, Oklahoma, and South Carolina) would vote; February 7, when Michigan and Washington state would vote; February 10, when Tennessee and Virginia would vote; February 24, when Hawaii, Idaho, and Utah would vote—but Super Tuesday, March 2, loomed as the date that would determine the Democratic Party nominee. On that day, ten states would vote: California, Connecticut, Georgia, Maryland, Massachusetts, Minnesota, New York, Ohio, Rhode Island, and Vermont. Still, to get to Super Tuesday, the candidates first had to compete in a string of primaries that were spaced together so closely it often seemed as if one primary had not ended before the race for the next one began.

On Thursday night in South Carolina, in the first debate after New Hampshire, the seven remaining candidates—Kerry, Dean, Edwards, Clark, Lieberman, Kucinich, and Sharpton—spent most of their time attacking Bush on a range of issues, among them the war in Iraq, terrorism, trade, and the economy. Dean was sensitive, now that it looked as if his campaign was heading for failure. "Everybody on this stage," he said, almost defensively, "or a lot of people on this stage have now embraced my message. They talk about change. They all talk about bringing people into the party. The truth is, I stood up for that message when nobody else would." That may have been true—at least it had been true enough to capture the attention of the media—but it had not translated into victories. The candidates ignored Dean's complaint. Instead, Kerry focused on reassuring the party that, should he win the nomination, he was going to run a national campaign. "I've always said I will compete in the South," he said. "I've always said I think I can win the South."

The next day, at a rally for veterans in South Carolina, Kerry explained how he would compete in the South. He would highlight his military record, and he would not hesitate to compare his military experience to that of Bush. "There are ninety-nine words in the State of the Union Address about steroid drug use in sports," Kerry said, "[but] the word 'veteran'—it doesn't appear once." Max Cleland, who was also on the stage with Kerry, made the attack against Bush personal. "We need a real deal, like John Kerry," he said, "not a raw deal, like what's in the White House now. We need somebody who felt the sting of battle, not someone who didn't even complete his tour stateside in the Guard." It was one of the most pointed attacks leveled against Bush's military service yet, but it was only the beginning of a debate about Bush and his duty in the National Guard.

On Saturday, the campaign took a weird turn when Dean launched a new attack on Kerry. *The Washington Post* ran an article documenting Kerry's relationships with corporate lobbyists. Dean then met with reporters on his bus in Arizona. Calling Kerry "a hand-maiden to special interests," he said: "Turns out we've got more than one Republican in the Democratic race. I've always said I thought Wes Clark was a Republican. Now apparently John Kerry has the same financing habits." According to Dean, if voters thought Kerry was a liberal from Massachusetts, they were wrong: Kerry was a Republican! In this same exchange with reporters, Dean addressed why his campaign was failing: "We got geared up for what we thought was going to be a frontrunner's campaign." In other words, from as far back as Labor Day, the overarching strategy of the Dean campaign had been predicated on a single flawed premise.

Kerry issued a statement through his campaign demanding Dean apologize for calling him a Republican, but the gesture was half-hearted. Kerry responded as lackadaisically as he did because, after his victories in Iowa and New Hampshire, he was enjoying himself on the campaign trail too much to let Dean get under his skin with name-calling. At a stop in Oklahoma on Saturday, Kerry was reciting his list of newly converted dignitaries who were endorsing him when a voice from the audience cried out. "Senator, I am the mayor of Watonga, Oklahoma, and I endorse you!" Stopping in mid-list, Kerry rushed off of the stage, found the mayor—his name was Richard Hightower—and pulled him onstage. Clasping hands with him, Kerry raised their arms aloft as if Hightower were his running mate and they were standing before the Democratic National Convention. "Ladies and gentlemen!" Kerry exclaimed triumphantly, "my latest endorsement!"

On Sunday, the Kerry campaign released a statement saying that it was running ads in all seven states voting on Little Super Tuesday and that Kerry would campaign in each state as well. On this day, Kerry received a key endorsement from the *St. Louis Post-Dispatch*, which called him "the best prepared Democratic candidate for president." He announced he would remain in North Dakota, where he was spending the day campaigning, to watch the Super Bowl on television that night, since his hometown team, the New England Patriots, was playing against the Carolina Panthers.

Meanwhile, Dean, who appeared on *Meet the Press*, was stuck explaining why his campaign was in collapse. "We took a gamble and it didn't pay off," Dean said. It didn't help that in interview after interview Dean was forced to refer to his campaign in the past tense.

But the major development on Sunday occurred when Terry McAuliffe, the chairman of the Democratic National Committee, went on *This Week* with George Stephanopoulos and challenged Bush on the subject of his military record. "I look forward to that debate," McAuliffe said, "when John Kerry, a war hero with a chest full of medals, is standing next to George Bush, a man who was AWOL [in the National Guard]. George Bush never served in our military in our country. He didn't show up when he should have shown up." McAuliffe made his comment within the larger context of Michael Moore's "deserter" comment, but the fact that a figure of such importance, the chairman of one of the two major political parties, was using a term as charged as "AWOL" only served to place Bush's military record at the center of a national debate.

The topic of Bush and the National Guard had a history to it, as McAuliffe knew when he made his comments on *This Week*. During the summer of 1999 and on into the presidential race in 2000, Bush was forced to deal with the charge that in 1968, his father, then a congressman from Texas, had pulled strings to get him into a Texas Air National Guard unit that had a waiting list with 150 names on it. This new controversy did not concern Bush's acceptance into the Guard, however, but what he did once he got in. During the spring of 1972, having served in his unit in Texas for four years, Bush asked to be transferred to a unit in Alabama, where he wanted to work on the Senate campaign of Winton "Red" Blount, a friend of the Bush family. Bush's application was denied, because the Alabama unit did not have airplanes and Bush was a pilot. "We met just one weeknight a month," a commander in the Alabama unit later told *The Boston Globe*. "We had no airplanes. We had no pilots."

Apparently, Bush violated orders and went to Alabama anyway. As of May of 1972, his attendance record at his Texas unit was nonexistent. When he failed to appear for a required medical exam, according to a report later published in the British newspaper *The Guardian*, the Texas Air National Guard banned him from flying. By the fall of 1972 he had made another application to transfer to a different unit in Alabama. This request was granted, and his superior officers assumed that he went to his new unit to continue his service. "His superiors," to quote *The Guardian*, "charged with writing an annual appraisal of Lieutenant Bush in May 1973, explained that he 'has not been observed at this unit during the period of report' because he was doing equivalent service in Alabama."

In fact, the records do not indicate satisfactorily that Bush performed his duty in Alabama as required under the "equivalent service" policy in the rules and regulations of the National Guard. His absence seemed to be substantiated by the fact that, despite the best efforts of journalists who interviewed contemporaries of Bush, few if any Guardsmen in either of the two Alabama units recalled Bush in any detail. As an adult, Bush, who said repeatedly during the 2000 race that his misbehavior in the past should be overlooked because "when I was young and irresponsible I was young and irresponsible," would refer to the period between the spring of 1972 and the spring of 1973 as his "lost year." He also said that he never failed to fulfill his duty in the National Guard, even in the lost year. However, when he ran for governor of Texas in 1994 and 1998 and when he ran for president in 2000, he had never released his full military file, so there was no hard proof of that fact.

On Monday, February 2, the day before Little Super Tuesday, Kerry was endorsed by the Sheet Metal Workers' International Association, a 150,000-member union with 150 locals—a huge boost to his already surging campaign. While he was campaigning in Albuquerque, New Mexico, Kerry was endorsed by Eliot Spitzer, the New York state attorney general. Also on Monday, on a Santa Fe–to–Phoenix flight, Dean told reporters he had read in the paper where he and Kerry would be campaigning the next day in Seattle. Dean suggested that, since he and Kerry were going to be in the same city on Tuesday, they should get together in Seattle on Monday night for a one-on-one debate, leaving out the other candidates, so that the voters would be able to size up the two main contenders in the race.

"Since we're both going to be there, maybe we should have a little election-eve debate," Dean said. "John's excuse was that he was too busy." Dean was referring to yet another challenge to a one-on-one debate he had made recently that Kerry had turned down. "But I now find that we're both in the same city on the same night. What an opportunity!" Dean did not mention that, when Kerry had challenged him to a one-on-one debate in the autumn, as Kerry sank in the polls and the media anointed Dean as the presumptive nominee, Dean had refused, claiming that it would be unfair to the other candidates. Nor did Dean mention that when Kerry challenged him again several weeks later, Dean had ignored him. On the flight to Phoenix, Dean did reflect, when he was asked to do so by reporters, on the current state of his campaign. "It's just the same as it was a year ago," Dean said. "Just put one foot in front of the other and keep going."

Putting one foot in front of the other became harder for Dean after Little Super Tuesday. By the end of the night, Kerry had won five of the seven elections being held that day, most of them by impressive margins. He won the primaries in Arizona, Delaware, Missouri, and New Mexico, as well as the caucus in North Dakota. The candidate who had once been criticized as "too regional"—read "Massachusetts liberal"—had won in the East, in the West, in the North, and on the border of the South in Missouri, sure to be a battleground state in the fall. The numbers were impressive: In Missouri, Kerry won with 51 percent of the vote; Edwards mustered only 25 percent. In Delaware, Kerry pulled in 50 percent. In Arizona, his 43 was followed by Clark with 27. "I am ready for this mission," Kerry said at a victory rally in Seattle. "From standing up to Richard M. Nixon to stopping George Bush and the Big Oil companies from drilling in the Alaska wildlife refuge, I know how to take on those powerful interests. I've done it all my life. I pledge to you tonight, I have just begun to fight." When he talked to reporters later in the evening, he seemed overwhelmed by the scope of his victory. "It's a huge night," he said. "I'm stunned by it."

On this night, Kerry lost to Edwards in South Carolina, where he finished second, and he lost in Oklahoma, where he came in third behind Clark and Edwards, who ended up in a virtual tie. (First place went to Clark, but only by a slim margin.) Edwards had been born in South Carolina, and Kerry decided it would be foolish to try to defeat Edwards in his home state, so he all but abandoned his South Carolina campaign. In Oklahoma, Edwards pulled in 30 percent of the vote, as did Clark, who in the end received only 1,216 more votes, which gave him the victory, if narrowly. Kerry took 27 percent. Clark was able to eke out a victory because he had been endorsed at the eleventh hour by Barry Switzer, the former head football coach of the Oklahoma Sooners who had become a legend in the state. On the whole, Clark had not done badly for the night, posting second-place finishes in Arizona, New Mexico, and North Dakota; however, in South Carolina, where he was supposed to do well, he came in fourth. "As an old soldier from Arkansas," he said in his victory celebration at the Oklahoma City Convention Center, "I could not be any prouder of your support in this first election that I have ever won."

One loser of the night was Joe Lieberman, who skipped Iowa, lost New Hampshire, and gambled his future on doing well in Delaware, where he finished a distant second to Kerry and essentially tied with Edwards, Dean, and Clark. On Primary Night, he stood before his supporters in a hotel ballroom in Arlington, Virginia, and announced his decision to withdraw from the race. He may have made history in 2000 by being the first Jewish American to be on a national ticket, but in the 2004 race, the disinterest of the electorate had become obvious. "The judgment of the voters is now clear," he said. "But for me it is now time to make a difficult but realistic decision. After looking at the returns and speaking with my family and my campaign team, I have decided tonight to end my quest for the presidency."

The cryptic comments Dean had been making to reporters about his campaign's strategy were more easily understood on the evening of Little Super Tuesday. It became apparent that the Dean campaign had been built on the notion that he would win Iowa and New Hampshire and then have so much momentum that he would win in the states that followed. It was, in fact, the slingshot strategy, using two states instead of one. When the early victories didn't materialize, Dean had no plans for how he would compete in the subsequent races, such as Little Super Tuesday. Dean had such weak organizations in these seven states that he did not even bother to campaign actively, focusing instead on future states where he might have a chance, among them Washington and Wisconsin. So, on Little Super Tuesday, Dean finished no better than third, with no more than 16 percent of the vote, in any of the seven races.

To downplay what was going to be an especially bad night, Dean spent the day campaigning outside the states that were voting. He didn't plan anything that might resemble a rally where he would have to give a concession speech. Instead, early in the evening before the results were obvious, be met with a group of supporters in Tacoma, Washington, and prepared the Deaniacs across the country for what was about to happen. "Well, the votes are starting to come in," he said, "and we're going to have a tough night tonight. But you know what? Here's why we're going to keep going and going and going and going and going, just like the Energizer Bunny. We're going to pick up some delegates tonight, and this is all about who gets the most delegates in Boston in July, and it's going to be us."

On Wednesday, the day on which Kerry was endorsed by the 1.3-million-member American Federation of Teachers, he stood before an audience in a town-hall meeting in Portland, Maine, and did something that, only a few months earlier when he could still get bogged down in Senatespeak, would have been unthinkable for him. As he discussed health care, instead of launching into a lecture about proposed legislation and the committees needed to pass it, he spoke about the illnesses of his parents in an almost confessional way.

One of the developments that had taken place after November, once Jeanne Shaheen and Mary Beth Cahill had secured their positions as key advisers, was a willingness on Kerry's part to try to connect with audiences on a human level. He did so today.

"I have seen the health care system at great length," he said. "I saw the administrative hassles, the problems, the things you run into, and I remember what it's like to be told, in a rehab hospital, 'Uh, well, we're sorry to tell you this, but tomorrow your Medicare runs out, and you've got to decide what you're going to do about your mother.' Now, in our family's case, we're very lucky. We're able to afford to get alternatives—difficult as it was, if I may say. It was hard to find the people, hard to line them up, and extraordinarily expensive. For most families in America, they don't have that choice. Most families in America say, 'What do we do? Sell the home? Dig into all our savings?' There goes what money would be left for the grandchildren. It's gone! You have to go into poverty to get care."

Audiences, like this one in Maine, could appreciate Kerry's growth as a candidate, unlike the national press corps, who remained infatuated with Dean. Kerry's confidants saw the growth as well. "Once Mary Beth took over, Kerry was able to focus on being a candidate," David Wade says. "That's when he started to come into his own as a campaigner."

On Thursday, Dean sent out a blanket e-mail to his donor base saying he needed to win the Wisconsin primary on February 17. The message was none too subtle: send money now. He summed up his e-mail, after he had asked for a $50 donation, with this proclamation: "The entire race has come down to this: we must win Wisconsin. Anything less will put us out of this race." As had happened for months, no sooner had the e-mail gone out than the money started pouring in. Even as they faced the grim prospect that Dean's campaign was falling apart, the Deaniacs held onto their hope that some-how Dean would be able to get his campaign on track, advance his cause, and win.

With the Michigan and Washington state primaries approaching on Saturday, Kerry met with fifty African-American ministers at the Second Ebenezer Baptist Church in Detroit. Then he took time out to meet in Boston with his deputy campaign manager, Steve Elmen-dorf, and union officials from whom Kerry was seeking endorse-ments. He had especially targeted the Teamsters, with whom Elmendorf had a good relationship. While the union endorsements were still up in the air, Elmendorf landed one on Friday that was easy for him: that of his old boss, Richard Gephardt. In a banquet hall near Detroit, Gephardt endorsed Kerry as they stood on a stage sur-rounded by teachers and firefighters. "I'm here today adding my voice to all of yours," Gephardt said. "I've known and worked with John Kerry for a long time. And when you campaign with and against someone, you even learn more about him. We want and need this man to be the next President of the United States." Now that he had won all but two of the contests, party luminaries were climbing on board a bandwagon that a mere three weeks ago didn't even exist.

On Saturday, February 7, Kerry won Michigan and Washington. Dean was a distant second in both races. In Michigan, the totals were Kerry 52 percent of the vote, Dean 17, and Edwards 14. In Wash-ington, Kerry got 49 percent of the vote, Dean 30, and Edwards 7. Kerry had now won nine out of the eleven contests, most of them by a healthy margin. Dean had not won one. "In Michigan and Wash-ington," Kerry said at a rally on Saturday night in Richmond, Virginia, "a message is being sent—and it's the same message that was sent from Iowa, to New Hampshire, to Missouri, to North Dakota, to New Mexico, to Arizona. And it is the message that I am carrying to Virginia and to Tennessee, and the message is: George Bush's days are numbered."

Even before he lost on Saturday night, Dean got more bad news. A new poll in Wisconsin showed that not only had he fallen behind, he was a distant third following Kerry and Clark. Dean was polling at only eight percent—an alarmingly small number—so he should not have been shocked when Gerald McEntee, president of the American Federation of State, County, and Municipal Employees, told him at lunch in Burlington that his union was withdrawing its endorsement. In the one-hour lunch, to which Dean was accompanied by Roy Neel, McEntee told Dean that, because he had come to believe Dean was not electable, he did not want to compromise the ability of another Democrat to win in the fall. Dean was hurt by the reversal; although McEntee didn't say it, he was bailing out on Dean because he had aspirations of his own. It was known in union circles that McEntee had designs on one day running the AFL-CIO. By tying his fortunes to a losing candidate, he was compromising his own political ambitions, as well.

Maine held its caucus on Sunday, February 8, with Kerry winning with 50 percent of the vote. Dean received 25 percent, Kucinich 15. Edwards and Clark were also-rans. Dean lost the state even though he appeared in person at numerous caucuses and greeted personally at least one in five of the voters who participated. Under state law, candidates can go to caucuses in person—and they often do. Kucinich also made appearances; in some caucuses, he spoke just before Dean. Kerry sent as a surrogate Robert Kennedy, Jr., who appeared at several caucuses. Kerry was not in Maine because he was campaigning in Virginia, where Governor Mark Warner endorsed him that morning in a ceremony outside the Governor's Mansion before they attended church services together in Richmond. Later in the day, when he had been declared the winner in Maine, Kerry released a statement, saying, "Today the voters of Maine have sent a message that . . . change is coming to America." The Dean camp could not help noting that the rhetoric Kerry was beginning to use sounded more and more like what Dean had been saying since he started his presidential campaign two years before.

In Nashville, that Sunday, a rally was being held for Tennessee Democrats, with both Edwards and Clark appearing at the event, but the main attraction, at least as far as advance buzz was concerned, was Al Gore. In what had been billed as a call to arms for Democrats, Gore made Bush the target of a direct partisan attack. "He betrayed this country!" Gore said. "He played on our fears. He took America on an ill-conceived foreign adventure, dangerous to our troops, an adventure preordained and planned before 9/11 ever took place." While Gore criticized the man who had defeated him in 2000, he seemed to back away slightly from the man he had endorsed in the current campaign. According to *The New York Times*, "[Gore] said he appreciated that Dr. Dean 'spoke forthrightly' against the war in Iraq, brought new people into the party and inspired the grass roots over the Internet. But Mr. Gore told the crowd that at an earlier reception for Dr. Dean, who was in Maine, he had said that no matter who won Tennessee on Tuesday, 'any one of these candidates is far better than George W. Bush.'"

The next day, February 9, Kerry received yet another endorsement, this one from the Amalgamated Transit Union, a 180,000-member union that had backed Gephardt while he was in the race. This was the eighth national labor union to endorse Kerry, who, as the frontrunner, was picking up support that had gone to Gephardt and Dean. On Tuesday, February 10, Kerry rolled up victories in two key southern states, Tennessee and Virginia. In both races, Edwards, who had based a good part of his campaign on the fact that he was a Southerner who would appeal to the South, placed a solid second. In Virginia, Kerry received 52 percent of the vote, with Edwards getting 27 percent, Clark 9, and Dean 7. In Tennessee, the race was only slightly closer, with Kerry pulling in 41 percent, Edwards 26, Clark 23, and Dean 4. At his victory rally at George Mason University in Fairfax, Virginia, Kerry played up his ability to win in the South, since he had been criticized early in the race as being too liberal to appeal to Southern voters. "Once again," Kerry said to the audience, "the message rings out loud and clear. Americans are voting for change—East and West, North, and now in the South."

The casualty of the day was Wesley Clark, who said through his communications director that he was withdrawing from the race. He would make a formal announcement in Little Rock the next day. Clark had gotten into the race late, he had skipped Iowa, but he was banking on attracting the attention of voters in his native South. His miserable showings on Monday had proved this hope unfounded.

On Tuesday, February 10, under pressure to address the speculation about Bush's National Guard service, the White House released papers intended to prove that he had not gone AWOL during the twelve-month period between May of 1972 and May of 1973. The documentation consisted of pay records confirming that Bush had performed his National Guard duty during the year in question. In total, from May until the end of the year, Bush was paid for nine days of active service, including six days in October and November of 1972 when he was assigned to the 187th Tactical Reconnaissance

Group in Alabama. However, the records confirmed that from mid-April until late October of 1972, a period of almost six months, Bush was not paid for any Guard duty at all. This would have been the time when he was in Alabama. Apparently, Bush lived in Alabama from May until November in 1972 (and probably longer) as he worked on Winton Blount's campaign. He had received permission to transfer to the Alabama Guard and, Bush said, he had reported for duty there.

But the pay stubs meant to help substantiate Bush's claim only called it into question further. If he had reported for duty during that six-month period, he would have been paid for it. To complicate matters, no records existed from the National Guard in Alabama to prove that Bush had reported for duty. In fact, the pay stubs showing Bush had been paid for two days in October and four days in November did not indicate where he had reported for duty on those days. According to the pay records, in the winter of 1973, Bush was back in Texas at least for part of the time. He was paid for six days in January, no days in February and March, two in April, fourteen in May, five in June, and nineteen in July. Then, even though he had six months left of his commitment to the National Guard, he was honorably discharged so that he could attend Harvard Business School starting in the fall. He "worked it out with the military," as Bush would one day say. How he worked it out with the military was never made clear.

On February 12, *The New York Times* reported that "the [developments] this week deepen a mystery that first surfaced during the 2000 presidential campaign when *The Boston Globe* reported that there was no record that Mr. Bush showed up for Guard drills between May 1972, when he moved to Alabama from Texas to work on a U.S. Senate race, and May 1973. Mr. Bush had been ordered in September 1972 to report for 'equivalent training' to William R.

Turnipseed, the 187th's deputy commander of operations, but the *Globe* quoted Mr. Turnipseed in 2000 as saying that Mr. Bush never reported to him. . . . In response to the *Globe*'s article, Mr. Bush's election campaign appealed for members of the Alabama Air National Guard to come forward and vouch for his service, and a group of Vietnam veterans in Alabama offered a $1000 reward for anyone with proof that Mr. Bush served. No one has come forward."

Nor was the White House able to end the debate on February 13, when the Bush Administration released Bush's dental records, which showed that he had received a routine dental exam at Dannelly Air National Guard Base in Montgomery, Alabama, in January of 1973. That still did not explain the six-month gap in 1972, although it did confirm that Bush had reported for duty in January, a month for which he was paid for six days of service. When reporters asked Kerry what he thought about the controversy involving Bush and his National Guard service as it was then developing, Kerry said, "It's not an issue that I chose to create."

Around this time, a picture surfaced that suggested just how much Vietnam would figure in the upcoming presidential race. In the photograph, a blurry, barely recognizable image of Kerry can be seen in a huge crowd of people sitting on the ground at an antiwar rally called Operation RAW (Rapid American Withdrawal) on September 7, 1970, in Valley Forge, Pennsylvania. Sitting two rows in front of Kerry, perfectly in focus, is Jane Fonda, staring thoughtfully at the speaker. The picture did not reveal any particular closeness, only that they had attended the same antiwar protest in 1970, two years before Fonda made her trip to Hanoi where she broadcast anti-American comments over the radio and became known as "Hanoi Jane."

The picture first appeared on a Web site run by Ted Sampley called vietnamveteransagainstjohnkerry.com. Sampley—a right-wing veteran activist—bought the picture for $179, from a source whose identity was not revealed, and posted it on the site. Soon, the shot was picked up by other sites. Then, on Thursday, February 12, it was published in papers across the country. Its caption in the *New York Post* read, "This photo of John Kerry and Jane Fonda at a Vietnam protest could cause him trouble," and the accompanying article's lead warned, "Democratic frontrunner John Kerry's past as an anti–Vietnam War activist came back to haunt him yesterday when a photo surfaced of Kerry with actress Jane Fonda at a 1970 protest rally."

On Wednesday, in an effort to kill the story before it gained momentum, Fonda had appeared on CNN, the news network owned by her ex-husband, Ted Turner, and tried to put distance between Kerry and activities she was involved in at the time. "Any attempt to link Kerry to me and make him look bad with that connection is completely false," she said. "We were at a rally for veterans at the same time. I spoke. Donald Sutherland spoke. John Kerry spoke"—so did George McGovern, Edmund Muskie, and Bella Abzug—"[but] I don't even think we shook hands."

By Thursday, as the picture of Kerry and Fonda hit the papers, a new picture was making the rounds on the Internet. In this one, Fonda is standing at a microphone and Kerry is holding a notepad, but, unlike the previous picture, they are standing next to each other. There was only one problem with the picture. According to Corbis, the photo agency that owned the original shot, the picture was a fraud. In the original, Kerry is standing by himself. Whoever doctored the picture had inserted the image of Fonda to make it appear as if she were standing next to him at the time the pictured was taken, when in fact she was not.

Soon, Kerry's attacker, Ted Sampley, was attacked himself—by John McCain, who described Sampley as "one of the most despicable people I have ever had the misfortune to encounter." McCain had cause to dislike Sampley for reasons beyond the fact that for years Sampley had criticized him over issues concerning American MIAs and POWs. Years back, Sampley had described McCain as "the Manchurian candidate," implying that he had been brainwashed by the North Vietnamese while he was held in captivity in the Hanoi Hilton. According to the theory, McCain was working as an agent for the communists now. In 1993, Sampley was found guilty of misdemeanor assault as a result of an incident where he attacked an aide to McCain, for which he was sentenced to 180 days of probation.

At the very time that the two Vietnam stories were developing— Did Bush go AWOL? Did Kerry consort with Fonda?—a new scandal erupted. On Thursday, February 12, Matt Drudge posted a self-reported story on his Web site stating that five media outlets were investigating "the nature of a relationship" between Kerry and "a woman who recently fled the country." Drudge offered no evidence of the investigations, let alone of a relationship between Kerry and the young woman, Alexandra Polier. Within minutes, Rush Limbaugh was talking about the story on his national radio show, and the media explosion had begun. By Friday, the story was in newspapers around the world; it got play in American papers, but it was featured prominently in the British tabloids. "I think he's a sleazeball," Polier's father, Terry, told one British reporter. "I did kind of wonder if my daughter didn't get that kind of feeling herself. He's not the sort of guy I would choose to be with my daughter. . . . John Kerry called my daughter and invited her down to Washington two or three years ago. He invited her to be on his reelection committee. She talked to him and decided against it." In this same article, Polier's mother, Donna, was quoted as saying she believed Kerry was "after" Alexandra.

On Friday morning, Kerry called in to Don Imus's morning radio show to deny the rumors, saying, "There's nothing to report, there's nothing to talk about. I'm not worried about it—no. The answer is no." Then, Kerry told a group of reporters from his traveling press corps that the allegations were "untrue." He added: "I just deny it categorically. It's rumor. It's untrue. Period. . . . And that's the last time I intend to [deny the allegations]."

Finally, on Monday, February 16, Alexandra Polier, who was identified as being 27 years old, issued a statement to the Associated Press from Nairobi, Kenya, where she was visiting the family of her fiancé, Yaron Schwartzman. "I have never had a relationship with Senator Kerry," Polier said, "and the rumors in the press are completely false. Whoever is spreading these rumors and allegations does not know me, but should know the pain they have caused me and my family. Because these stories were false, I assumed the media would ignore them. It seems that efforts to peddle these lies continue, so I feel compelled to address them." She said she had never worked for Kerry, as had been suggested in some reports. She graduated from Clark University in Worcester, Massachusetts, in 1999, received a master's degree in journalism from Columbia University in 2003, and landed an editorial-assistant position at the Associated Press after that.

On Monday, Polier's parents issued their own statement. "We have spoken to our daughter," they said, "and the allegations that have been made regarding her are completely false and unsubstantiated. We appreciate the way Senator Kerry has handled the situation and intend on voting for him for president of the United States."

As these controversies played out, the political process continued. On February 11, in a departure from what he had said on his Web site to raise money, Dean was quoted as saying, "We're going on from Wisconsin, win or lose." Then, on February 13, Wesley Clark endorsed Kerry. At a rally in the armory building on the campus of the University of Wisconsin in Madison, Kerry was onstage before a crowd when Clark approached. "Sir," Clark said in his best military voice, "request permission to come aboard! The army is here!"

"President Bush hasn't led America," Clark said, "he's misled America. . . . [I will do] everything I can to help when the Republican mean machine cranks up their attacks." As for Kerry, Clark said, "I ask you to join me in standing up for an American who has given truly outstanding service to his country in peace and in war."

Kerry campaigned in Wisconsin before he headed to Nevada, where caucuses would be held the next day. With the Clark endorsement, he spent part of the day answering questions about a subject he wanted to avoid at all costs: whom he would pick as his running mate. Would Clark make a good one? (After all, according to press reports, Dean had "dangled," to quote *The New York Times,* the vice presidency in front of Clark last summer.) What about John Edwards? Other names were beginning to be floated, such as Senator Evan Bayh of Indiana, Governor Bill Richardson of New Mexico, and the two senators from Florida, Bob Graham and Bill Nelson. But Kerry was careful. He would not make a public display of the selection process the way Gore had when it was made known that Gore's short list consisted of John Edwards, Joe Lieberman, and Kerry. "We were notified by one of Gore's legal team who was doing the vetting," David McKean says about the process that took place in the summer of 2000. "Would he be interested in pursuing it? And John said yes, he would be. He turned over basically every sort of piece of written material to this legal team, and then John was questioned on, I think, a couple of occasions by them. Ultimately he had an interview at the vice president's home." According to an anonymous source, the interview was odd. "Gore handled the interview like Kerry was applying for a job at a bank. Gore had a legal pad and sort of went down a checklist, marking things off with a pen. Not an intimate conversation at all. The whole thing was strange." Or as McKean says: "Kerry came back and felt that it had gone fine, but that, as he put it, he and Gore didn't wind up sitting on the floor, chatting for hours, the way Clinton and Gore had eight years earlier. He wasn't wildly optimistic after his session with Gore."

Reporters claimed at the time that Kerry was so sure he was Gore's choice that he had already started writing his acceptance speech. Given the way he perceived his meeting and described it to others, this was unlikely. Still, when he was asked by *The Boston Globe* to comment on the selection of Lieberman, he said, "I'd be a liar if I didn't say to you there's a little disappointment." One night not long after, Kerry and Edwards had dinner together at Olive's, a restaurant not far from the White House—one of the few times the two men had socialized during their years together in the Senate.

"Kerry and Edwards were not social friends," McKean says. "Edwards hadn't been in the Senate very long. John liked him and thought he was a bright guy. In general, John socializes with some of his colleagues, but not that many. Mostly, he has dinner with his wife when their schedules permit."

On Saturday, February 14, Kerry won the Nevada caucus with 63 percent of the vote; Dean got 17 percent, Edwards 10, and Kucinich 7. Kerry also won the race in Washington D.C. The totals were Kerry 47 percent, Sharpton 20, Dean 17. On Sunday, Steven Grossman, Dean's campaign chairman, told reporters, "If Howard Dean does not win the Wisconsin primary, I will reach out to John

Kerry unless he reaches out to me first. I will make it clear that I will do anything and everything I can to help him become the next president, and I will do anything and everything I can to build bridges with the Dean organization."

Grossman had history with Kerry. He had known him for thirty years and had served as chairman of his Senate campaign in 1996. He was also a past chairman of the Democratic National Committee, so he knew what he was doing when he made his comments. Dean did, too, and he responded to a local Fox affiliate in Wisconsin. "We're not dropping out after Tuesday, period," he said, totally contradicting what he had said in the e-mail he had sent out asking for money to win Wisconsin. Maybe Dean had no plans to drop out, but his campaign now appeared as if it were in fatal decline. He only had enough money to run one ad in Wisconsin, he had stopped polling, and he had not lined up any campaign events after the Wisconsin primary. Dean was returning to Burlington to map out his future strategy. Still, when Dean said through a spokesman, about Grossman, "We'll miss him and we wish him well," it was obvious that he was not interested in listening to what Grossman had to say. In fact, he was dismissing Grossman even before he officially had an offer to join Kerry.

That Sunday, President Bush appeared at the Daytona 500. His father had gone to the event twelve years before when he was running for reelection. Wearing a NASCAR sweatshirt, Bush said, "Gentlemen, start your engines!" and then left. That night, during a debate between the remaining Democratic candidates in Milwaukee, Bush was a frequent target. But, when Kerry was asked if, in the general election, he or someone in the party, like Terry McAuliffe, would make an issue out of whether or not Bush went AWOL, Kerry said, "I don't plan to do that, and I've asked them not to."

On the day before the Wisconsin primary, *The Milwaukee Journal Sentinel,* the state's largest newspaper, endorsed John Edwards in a surprise move, arguing, "He may have the stronger legs in this long-distance race." On Monday, Steve Grossman, following the drama of the day before, joined the Kerry campaign. Grossman put it this way: "I think it's fair to assume my public statements and actions are tantamount to a resignation." Dean said he bore him "no ill will at all," but on the Dean Web site people writing in had taken to calling Grossman "Judas."

At campaign stops during the day, Dean was obviously angered by Grossman's departure, but he vowed to keep going. In Madison, when the crowd started chanting, "We want Dean," Dean, clearly peeved, responded, "Well, if you vote for him, you'll have him." Finally, at one point in all of this, Dean snapped at reporters, "Let me remind you all that I have more delegates than everyone else in this race except John Kerry." This was true; he had amassed a number of "super" delegates, party and elected officials who can pledge unbinding support to a candidate during the primary season. The current delegate count was (with 2,162 needed to win): Kerry 577, Dean 188, and Edwards 166. "So," Dean continued, "I think the campaign obituaries that some of you have been writing are a little misplaced.... John Edwards said the other day this is a two-person race. I would agree. It's a two-person race between me and John Kerry."

On Monday, Kerry crisscrossed the state in a last-ditch whirlwind effort. He had voted for the North American Free Trade Agreement in 1993—legislation hated in Wisconsin, a state known to be hospitable to labor unions, which was why Edwards was constantly reminding voters that Kerry had been in favor of it—so he had to spend much of his time explaining his vote. In general, Kerry argued that he was in favor of the concept of free trade but that he would have enforced NAFTA better than had the Bush Administration, which had overseen a historic shift in jobs from America to foreign countries. Edwards underscored Kerry's support of NAFTA. "There is a difference," Edwards said at a rally at the South Milwaukee Community Center. "There is a choice for Wisconsin voters on this issue. I'm against NAFTA, I was against NAFTA. Governor Dean and Senator Kerry were for it."

On Tuesday, the voters of Wisconsin did not hold Kerry's support for NAFTA against him. When the votes were counted, Kerry had 40 percent, Edwards 34; once again, Dean was a distant third. That evening became a battle of televised post-election speeches. In his speech, Edwards said, "The people of Wisconsin spoke loudly and clearly tonight. They want a debate. They want this campaign to continue."

The press began to characterize it as a two-man race between Edwards and Kerry and reported that members of Kerry's inner circle were startled that their candidate's victory was not more decisive. "That's not true," one says. "We never expected Kerry to do better in Wisconsin than he did. We were very happy with the results that night." Kerry, who had upstaged Edwards by coming out to start his speech before Edwards had finished his, forcing the television networks to cut away from Edwards to Kerry, went out of his way to sound upbeat. "The motto of the state of Wisconsin is 'Forward,'" he said. "I want to thank the state of Wisconsin for moving this cause and this campaign forward tonight." During his speech at the Madison Marriott West hotel, he alluded to one of President Kennedy's most famous lines when he said, in introducing his wife, "I'm getting to be the guy who accompanies Teresa around the United States of America, which is just fine by me."

Howard Dean spoke before a modest audience in a hotel ballroom in Madison, without acknowledging his third place finish. "We are not done yet," he said to the Deaniacs who had shown up. "You have already started to change the Democratic Party, and we will not stop. You have already written the platform of the Democratic Party for this election." He added: "We have a long way to go. In order to change America, we have to fundamentally change Washington, both the Democrats and the Republicans." Finally, he said: "We will change the Democratic Party, we will change America, and we will change the White House. Let's fight on. On Wisconsin. Keep up the fight for a better America. Never give up, never give up, never give up." Within the hour, Dean was on a jet flying home to Burlington.

The next day, Wednesday, February 18, Howard Dean suspended his campaign. In a hotel ballroom in Burlington, with Judy standing behind him onstage, he officially declared, "I'm no longer a candidate." Earlier, that morning, he had met with his staff at headquarters, after which he held a conference call with members of Congress who had supported him, a call in which he said he thought Edwards would make a stronger candidate than Kerry. Speaking in the ballroom, he avoided the issue of whom he would endorse. Instead, he spoke to his staff and supporters, some 250 of them, about what they had accomplished and what they would strive for in the future. "We are leaving one track," he said, "but we are going on another track that will take back America for ordinary people. . . . This is the end of Phase One of this fight, but the fight will go on, and we will be together in that fight. . . . We are not going away. We are staying together, unified, all of us." He said he was converting his campaign into a loosely defined political organization whose goal would be to defeat Bush in the general election. He concluded his speech with a line he had used over and over during the campaign: "You have the power to take our country back. And together we have the power to take back the White House in 2004. And that is exactly what we are going to do."

The numbers released by the campaign were striking. Just under 320,000 individuals had donated $50.3 million to his presidential campaign—one of the most impressive fund-raising efforts in the history of presidential politics. The tragedy, of course, was that the money had not been able to buy success. Immediately, the post-mortem began. One high-ranking Dean aide confessed to a journalist, "There was no decision-making process. There was no structure. There was no one in charge."

On Thursday, *The New York Times* ran an editorial entitled "Goodbye, Candidate Dean." It said in part: "[T]he principal survivors now left in the primary arena gained immeasurably from Dr. Dean's combative lead. He transplanted a spine into the presidential campaign. And Dr. Dean hardly hurt their chances by packing up his quest yesterday not with a whimper or a scream, but with a creative call to his followers to stay within Democratic ranks as a driving force for change. . . . Three months ago, before anyone voted, Dr. Dean was measured by some as an unstoppable phenomenon. Instead, his campaign turned out to be a humbling experience for pollsters, pundits, and, most of all, himself. In the wondrous variables of politics, Dr. Dean was ultimately not popular enough, anywhere he tried. But he will continue to shadow the Democrats' ongoing campaign as an object lesson in daring and tactical innovation."

The one development for which the Dean campaign will be remembered was its use of the Internet, and much about how it was used was inspired by Joe Trippi. To raise money, the campaign created, in effect, online telethons. The campaign would post how much money it needed to raise and the period of time it needed to raise it in, and then the money flowed in until the goal was met. The campaign introduced the blog to politics, and in so doing it created a sense of community within the Dean organization that would become central to its success. Through Meetup.com, Dean supporters conversed with one another about when and where they would hold gatherings in a way supporters of a candidate had never done before. Much of how Trippi and his staff used the Internet was brilliant and revolutionary—which was why Trippi pledged to set up his own independent political action committee in the future—but in the end the Dean campaign went bust in just as spectacular a way as so many dot-com companies did during the late 1990s. The Dean campaign as dot-com startup—not a comparison the campaign would have appreciated, especially during its salad days when it seemed that Howard Dean was going to coast to the nomination with little if any competition.

"The media crowned Howard Dean as the nominee, and he couldn't handle that kind of pressure," Roger Stone says. "His campaign just imploded." Or as Mary Beth Cahill puts it: "Dean got an enormous amount of attention and, for a long time, no scrutiny. When the scrutiny accompanied the attention, his campaign wasn't ready for it." Former Clinton aide Sidney Blumenthal says, "Dean was inexperienced in national politics. He had never been the subject of so much intense scrutiny and criticism, not from the press so much as from other people in politics. And he withered under it. He saw this as being about himself and became entangled in the whole imbroglio. As a result, he descended into a tit-for-tat negative campaign with Gephardt; lost his overarching message; didn't develop his themes; lost the sense of what his campaign was about; and allowed Kerry to walk around his very dead body."

In the days after the Wisconsin primary, Kerry's campaign agenda was determined by the press corps' depiction of the ongoing battle for the party's nomination. Edwards had only 190 delegates, and a slim chance to win enough to threaten Kerry's lead, but the media was determined to create the story of a two-man race between them, whether or not one existed. In fact, the media had completely missed the real story of the 2004 presidential nomination process. During September, October, and November, when Kerry, Dean, Edwards, and the rest of the Democratic field were driving the back roads of Iowa and weathering the snowstorms of New Hampshire, the majority of the national media, and especially television coverage, all but ignored the race. People in power at the networks did not understand that, in this presidential cycle more than in almost any before it, the primary and caucus season had been front-loaded so heavily that as early as January—and no later than March—the Democratic Party would have its nominee. In previous contests, the nominee would typically not emerge until well in the process—April or May; even June, which tended to happen back in the 1960s and 1970s.

When Kerry won Iowa, New Hampshire, and five of the seven primaries and caucuses held on February 3, the contest was virtually over—but that did not keep producers, editors, and journalists from trying to keep the process alive. First, there was the story, more or less fabricated, of the two-man race between Dean and Kerry. When Dean dropped out after his third-place finish in Wisconsin, the media had to invent another two-man race. This one, *totally* fabricated, pitted Edwards against Kerry. Some early tracking polls in New York and California showed Kerry ahead of Edwards by as many as 50 percentage points, but these drew little coverage. The reality of the numbers was inconvenient to the story, so the numbers were ignored.

"This was so annoying at the time," one Kerry staffer says. "I mean, the race in Wisconsin was not that close. Then to use that as the basis for a two-way race, when we were ahead of Edwards by landslide margins in the key states, was ludicrous."

On Thursday, the 19th, despite the way the national media was portraying the race, the Kerry bandwagon rolled on as John Sweeney, president of the AFL-CIO, formally endorsed Kerry from the steps of the union's headquarters in Washington. "This is a man," Sweeney said to the union members gathered in front of the hall, "who will not sign his name to a single trade agreement that does not include worker protections and environmental protections." Then Kerry talked about the laid-off workers who, hit hard by "the Bush economy," had come up to him at events across the country to tell him their stories. "They have touched my conscience and my heart," he said. "I will never forget them. I will be a president who fights for those workers."

Meanwhile, on the very day one of the country's largest unions was endorsing Kerry, the leader of another union, the Federation of State, County, and Municipal Employees, was making news for a comment he made about Dean. Gerald McEntee told a reporter that, not long before he withdrew his union's support of Dean, he decided Dean was "nuts." "I go to Burlington," McEntee said, "and I meet with [Dean]. I'm telling you, I threw more ice water on his head in about twenty-five minutes than probably he has ever had. And I said: 'Don't do Wisconsin, okay? Don't go in.' I told him to get out. I said, 'You can't win.' He said he's still going into Wisconsin. I said: 'We're not. We're off the train. If you think I'm going to spend a million dollars to get you another point after this election is over, you're crazy.'"

On Saturday morning, in a conference call with reporters arranged by the Bush reelection staff, Saxby Chambliss, who had defeated Max

Cleland in the midterm election, claimed that Kerry was weak on military issues. "When you have a thirty-two-year history of voting to cut defense programs and cut defense systems," Chambliss told the reporters, "folks in Georgia are going to look beyond what he says and look at his voting record." As soon as Kerry learned about the call, he got angry. He vented while he was campaigning in Atlanta. "I don't know what it is," he said, "that these Republicans who didn't serve in any war have against those of us who are Democrats who did." Charging that Bush had "initiated a widespread attack" on him during the past week, Kerry wrote Bush a letter, which he both sent to him and then released to the media late Saturday night. In it, Kerry accused Bush of trying to smear him on the issue of the military and challenged him to a one-on-one debate about the Vietnam era and the way each had lived his life during that time. "As you well know," Kerry wrote, "Vietnam was a very difficult and painful period in our nation's history, and the struggle for our veterans continues. So it has been hard to believe that you would choose to reopen these wounds for your personal political gain. But, that is what you have chosen to do. . . . America deserves a better debate. If you want to debate the Vietnam era, and the impact of our experiences on our approaches to presidential leadership, I am prepared to do so. . . . This is not a debate to be distorted through your $100 million campaign fund. This is a debate that should be conducted face to face."

On Sunday, Kerry attended services in Atlanta at the Ebenezer Baptist Church, where Martin Luther King, Jr., had preached. Kerry did not speak, but sat in the congregation and listened to the Reverend Dr. Joseph L. Roberts, Jr., tell the audience that they needed to know about Kerry's "vast experience in foreign policy, about the fact that he turned down the Appropriations Committee to work in foreign policy—and certainly, if anything is in need of assistance, it is America's posture in foreign policy."

As the minister delivered his sermon, Ralph Nader, the activist who many people believe cost Al Gore the election in 2000, was making news on *Meet the Press*, announcing that he was going to run for president again in 2004. This time, there would be one difference. In 2000, when he received 2.7 percent of the vote, Nader had run as the nominee of the Green Party. In 2004, the Green Party was unavailable to him—perhaps the party didn't want to be the reason Bush got elected again—so Nader was running as an independent. He tried to justify his campaign to Tim Russert and in a series of print interviews he did on Sunday for Monday publication. "This campaign," he told *USA Today*, "will help beat Bush because we can expose the Bush regime's vulnerabilities and failures in additional, effective ways that the Democrats are too cautious or too indentured to corporations to do by themselves."

On Monday, February 23, eight days before Super Tuesday, Kerry traveled to New York City, specifically the Alhambra Ballroom in Harlem, only a few blocks away from Bill Clinton's postpresidential offices, where he received the endorsement of, among others, Congressman Charles Rangel of New York. Rangel, at the urging of friends of the Clintons if not the Clintons themselves, had been an early supporter of Wesley Clark. Before a mostly African-American crowd, Rangel now pledged his support to Kerry.

The news of the day centered around whether or not the Bush reelection team had used the term "Operation Carpet-bombing" to describe a negative-ad assault that, according to Kerry, was slated to begin soon. On a conference call with reporters on Monday, Marc Racicot, the chairman of the Republican National Committee, denied the charge. The use of such a name, he said, would be outrageous, "particularly in the presently existing context." But the Kerry camp stood by their claims, even though Kerry's aides could not produce proof of anyone associated with Bush or his campaign using the name. David Wade said that Democrats, whom he did not identify, "and even Republican friends" had used the term. "If the term hasn't found its way into print," Wade wrote in an e-mail, "its distortions certainly have. From Rush Limbaugh to Sean Hannity to Laura Ingraham to Saxby Chambliss to the Republican National Committee, you can't turn on a TV or pick up a radio without seeing a systematic and coordinated attack on John Kerry."

This was true. Kerry's alleged sex scandal, the pictures of Kerry and Fonda (doctored or otherwise), Kerry and his medals and Vietnam in general—these topics provided endless fodder for the right-wing media. Then, on Monday, Bush himself entered the fray. Speaking at a fund-raiser for Republican governors, Bush said to the 1,400 people in attendance: "The action we take and the decisions we make in this decade will have consequences far into this century. If America shows weakness and uncertainty, the world will drift toward tragedy. That will not happen on my watch." Bush meant, of course, that while he was strong on security, Kerry, as president, would be weak. In case there was any doubt about to whom he was referring, Bush spelled it out when he joked: "The other party's nomination battle is still playing out. The candidates are an interesting group with diverse opinions. They're for tax cuts and against them. They're for NAFTA and against NAFTA. They're for the Patriot Act and against the Patriot Act. They're in favor of liberating Iraq, and opposed to it. And that's just one senator from Massachusetts."

Bush made the address—and delivered the speech—as a response to the negative feedback within his own party over his State of the Union Address and over a recent appearance on *Meet the Press*, where he had looked defensive and unsure of himself. So Bush hit the Republican red-meat issues hard. "It's a choice," he said, "between keeping the tax relief that is moving the economy forward, or putting the burden of higher taxes back on the American people. It's a choice between an America that leads the world with strength and confidence, or an America that is uncertain in the face of danger." At a White House event for the governors earlier in the day, Rodney Paige, the secretary of education, referred to the National Education Association, a group often affiliated with the Democratic Party, as "a terrorist organization" because the N.E.A. opposed certain portions of Bush's education legislation passed in 2001. It was the kind of language even jaded Washington insiders expressed shock at hearing, especially from a member of the president's cabinet.

On Tuesday, it was on to Ohio for Kerry. Launching what his press team called his "Jobs Tour," Kerry attended staged events at a manufacturing plant in Youngstown, toured a plant that had closed (the point here was to underscore the fact that under Bush the American economy had lost three million jobs), and held a spirited rally in Cleveland. The same day, in a five-minute speech delivered in the Roosevelt Room of the White House, Bush announced that he wanted a Constitutional amendment banning gay marriage, asserting that the union between a man and a woman is "the most fundamental institution of civilization." As he urged Congress to move quickly, Bush said he was forced to make such a request because of "activist judges." In a session in which he did not take questions from reporters, Bush summed up his position on the proposed amendment by saying, "The amendment should fully protect marriage while leaving the state legislatures free to make their own choices in defining legal arrangements other than marriage."

Kerry downplayed his response to Bush's announcement. Historically, Kerry had opposed gay marriage but supported civil unions, which he believed supplied the same legal protections. But Kerry saw Bush's announcement as an attempt to placate his right-wing voting base and polarize independent voters, so he decided not to let Bush dictate the debate on a subject that would probably remain hypothetical, since the odds of a Constitutional amendment passing into law were slim. Still, the shots fired from one side and returned by the other suggested that as early as February, it was becoming a two-man race: Bush versus Kerry.

That day, February 24, Kerry won three more races, in Hawaii, Utah, and Idaho. The totals in Utah, a state where he had never even campaigned (no one else did either), was not close: Kerry got 55 percent of the vote to Edwards's 30. Kerry also won the Idaho caucus with 64 percent of the vote to Edwards's 20. Kerry had used surrogates in the states—Henry Cisneros, the former Clinton cabinet member, in Utah; his wife and the singer-songwriter Carole King in Idaho. King was a longtime resident of Idaho, and Teresa owned a vacation home there.

On Wednesday, in Washington, Alan Greenspan, the chairman of the Federal Reserve, appeared before a session of the House Budget Committee and said that instead of increasing taxes (or rolling back any of the Bush tax cuts, even those for individuals making more than $200,000 a year), the federal government should cut spending on such programs as Social Security. "The crucial issue out here," Greenspan said, "is the rate of growth of the economy, and what history does tell us is that keeping tax rates down will tend to maximize that." Then Greenspan uttered a sentence that would have been political suicide if an elected official had said it: "A thorough review of our spending commitments—and at least some adjustments in those commitments—is necessary for prudent policy." He meant Social Security and Medicare. He also suggested raising the retirement age from 65 to 67.

Privately, Kerry aides were surprised that Greenspan would make the comments he did on the Hill. If there was one subject known to be off-limits to politicians, it was Social Security. But Kerry did not press the issue in public. Instead, he stuck to his game plan, and that meant giving a speech at the University of Toledo that was billed as a major economic address. As he did the day before, Kerry underscored the number of jobs lost during Bush's presidency; this had now become a refrain of the Kerry campaign. At this campaign stop, Kerry picked up the endorsement of former Democratic senator John Glenn, who made the point to the standing-room-only audience that in all of his years in politics he had never before endorsed a Democrat in a primary race—that was how disturbed he was by the direction in which the Bush Administration was taking the country.

That night, Kerry traveled to St. Paul, Minnesota, for a rally that was so heavily subscribed that 3,000 people were allowed into the gymnasium at Macalester College, but, on orders of the fire marshal, another 1,000 were turned away. Now it was former vice president Walter Mondale who filled the role of celebrity endorser.

On Thursday, Kerry learned of more endorsements from newspapers across the country. In addition to the *San Jose Mercury News* and the *Dayton Daily News,* he received the much-sought-after approval of *The New York Times.* After saying that he "exudes maturity and depth" on foreign affairs even as he developed campaign skills that were "pretty good and getting better," the *Times* went on: "His early campaign was disastrous, and his slip from favorite to also-ran was so dramatic as to be embarrassing. But he pulled his organization together and handily won the early primaries. . . . What his critics see as an inability to take strong, clear positions seems to us to reflect his appreciation that life is not simple. He understands the nuances and shades of gray in both foreign and domestic policy. . . . The search for a Democratic presidential nominee has been defined by an Anyone-but-Bush sentiment, an obsession with choosing the man who will run the best campaign. But in the end, the party needs to pick the person who is most qualified to be president. That's why this page endorses Senator John Kerry in Tuesday's primary."

This same day, February 26, Kerry flew from Minnesota to Los Angeles, where he was scheduled to appear with the other Democratic candidates at a debate sponsored by CNN and the *Los Angeles Times* and moderated by Larry King. The four remaining Democratic candidates—Kerry, Edwards, Kucinich, and Sharpton—arrived for their debate, which took place on the campus of the University of Southern California. At one point, Edwards described Kerry as "a good candidate" who would make "a good president." Likewise, Kerry called Edwards "an American story" although, he pointed out, "I've had experiences that John hasn't had. We all bring to the table our life." Because of what Bush had said about gay marriage early in the week, and because that day in San Francisco Rosie O'Donnell had married her girlfriend, Kelly Carpenter, the issue of gay marriage came up—Kerry restated his support for civil unions—but mostly the debate centered on the economy, Bush's shortcomings, and candidate electability.

After the debate, at a rally near the campus, Kerry received yet another endorsement, this one from former Governor Gray Davis, who, as a member of Kerry's traveling press corps was heard to quip, "may be the most unpopular politician in the state of California at the moment." In fact, when Kerry introduced him to the cheering crowd, Davis seemed genuinely moved that they were cheering, given the fact that he had recently lost a recall vote to Arnold Schwarzenegger. Working to maintain composure, Davis said to Kerry, "I was proud to serve with you," meaning in Vietnam. "I am ready to enlist in the Kerry army."

On the other side of the country, Howard Dean made his first public appearance since quitting the race eight days earlier when he showed up at the Omni Hotel near Yale University to speak at a thank-you rally for 500 of his workers. "You have revitalized politics," he said. "A lot of times people give up. . . . You can't afford to do that, because we are fortunate enough to live in a country where politics really matters. And politics from now on is going to be ours."

The next day, Kerry delivered a foreign-policy address at the University of California at Los Angeles. "As we speak," he said, "night has settled on the mountains of the border between Afghanistan and Pakistan. If Osama bin Laden is sleeping, it is the restless slumber of someone who knows his days are numbered. I don't know if the latest reports, saying that he is surrounded, are true or not. We've heard this news before. . . . We had him in our grasp more than two years ago at Tora Bora, but George Bush held U.S. forces back, and instead called on Afghan warlords with no loyalty to our cause to finish the job. We all hope the outcome will be different this time, and we all know America cannot rest until Osama bin Laden is captured or killed."

At the same time, Edwards had abandoned his day of campaigning in California when new polls showed that Kerry was going to win the state on Tuesday in a landslide. Instead, he headed for Minnesota, where he hoped he might fare better, but in reality the Edwards campaign was running out of steam.

After attending a fund-raiser in San Francisco, Kerry ended his day with a rally at a union hall in Oakland, where he was introduced by Dianne Feinstein, California's popular senator who had been one of the first members of Congress to endorse Kerry back in September. At the time, she looked as if she were out of step with her party; now she looked like what she was—a savvy politician with a keen eye for what voters want.

On the evening of Saturday, February 28, Kerry held a town-hall meeting in an auditorium of the Medgar Evers College in Crown Heights in Brooklyn. The overflow crowd of 500 was mostly African-American and Latino, and the response Kerry got was as warm and enthusiastic as any he had received on the recent campaign trail. For part of the meeting, he sat on a stool in front of a stage full of students and faculty members of the college. When he was not sitting down, he roamed the audience, microphone in hand, Donahue style, which had become a trademark of his campaign. Earlier that day, Kerry had received endorsements from Mario Cuomo, the former governor of New York, and his son Andrew, the former housing secretary under Clinton. But the highlight of the day was a small event that transpired at the town-hall meeting that night.

As part of the proceedings, the Kerry campaign—as always, the local staff had coordinated plans with Cahill's office in Washington—had lined up testimonials from people who were trying to triumph in a bad economy, including a 22-year-old East Harlem high-school dropout named Michael Parker. Parker was a member of Youth Build, a community-outreach program that had gotten some of its vital early funding in 1992 when Kerry discovered the program, became impressed with it, and put it into an appropriations bill.

Parker explained how Youth Build was helping him: with the assistance of the program, he had received his GED, and he was now lining up money to go to college. He was holding down a minimum-wage job in a drugstore so he could qualify for grants. For the first time in his life, he was hopeful about his future.

"I was one of those people you'd like to call a statistic," he said. He also talked about meeting Kerry through the program. "He's a cool brother," Parker said, much to Kerry's amusement. Then Parker summed up his remarks. "When I was young," Parker said, "my grandmother used to say, 'If it ain't broke, don't fix it.' " Parker paused and looked at Kerry, who stood beside him, listening. "Senator, this community is broke. Please fix it for us." Kerry was visibly moved by this remark. The audience started to applaud. One person stood, and then another, until all of the audience was standing. As they did, Kerry and Parker embraced. Then, when the ovation had ceased, Kerry said, "I think that was one of the most eloquent things I've ever heard."

It was the kind of moment on the campaign trail that, years ago, used to happen to another senator with Boston roots as he ran for president—Robert Kennedy—when the hope of a community had found its expression in the voice of a leader.

On the Sunday before Super Tuesday, Kerry spent most of the day in New York City. That morning, CBS News and *The New York Times* co-sponsored a debate between the remaining four candidates. It was the first time in recent debate appearances that Edwards, in a desperate effort to raise his profile with voters before Super Tuesday, made direct attacks on Kerry. Citing a *Washington Post* article that said Kerry would not be able to pay for his campaign promises, Edwards accused Kerry of engaging in "the same old Washington talk that people have been listening to for decades." People "want something different," Edwards argued.

"You should have learned not to believe everything you read in a newspaper," Kerry shot back.

During the debate, Kerry attempted to make amends to the Jewish community for questions he had raised about the fence that Israel was constructing along its borders to protect itself from attacks by militant supporters of the Palestinian cause. Making sure his position was clear, Kerry described the fence as being "necessary to the security of Israel until [the Israelis] have a partner to be able to negotiate [with]." Later in the day, Kerry met privately with Jewish leaders in New York to assure them that he supported Prime Minister Ariel Sharon and that, as he had said, he felt the main obstacle to peace was the fact that Israel did not have a partner with whom to negotiate. He specifically addressed the issue of Yasir Arafat, the chairman of the Palestinian Authority. In his book *The New War,* published in 1997, four years after the Oslo Accords were signed by Arafat and Yitzhak Rabin, Kerry had called Arafat a "statesman" and a "role model"—an opinion he no longer held after years of the Intifada and terror apparently sanctioned by Arafat; he now believed that, as he told the Jewish leaders, Arafat was no "partner in peace."

On the day before Super Tuesday, Kerry appeared at a rally at Morgan State University in Baltimore before an audience of 600, after which he proceeded to Atlanta for a nighttime rally where he received the endorsement of Mayor Shirley Franklin.

Finally, Super Tuesday arrived. By mid-afternoon, when the exit polls began to come in, it became clear that Kerry was going to get massive support across the board. If the voting patterns held up, it looked as if Kerry would win landslide victories in the major states of New York and California and do extremely well in most if not all of the other races.

As the polls closed, Kerry saw victory after victory. In California, he got 67 percent of the vote; his closest rival was Edwards with 18 percent. In New York, Kerry had 60 percent, Edwards 20. Kerry had similar advantages in Connecticut (Kerry 58 percent, Edwards 24), Maryland (Kerry 60 percent, Edwards 25), Minnesota (Kerry 51 percent, Edwards 27), Ohio (Kerry 52 percent, Edwards 34), and Rhode Island (Kerry 71 percent, Edwards 19). As expected, Massachusetts was a blowout: Kerry 72 percent, Edwards 18. The only race that was close was in Georgia, where Kerry got 47 percent to Edwards's 41, and the only state Kerry lost was Dean's home state of Vermont. There, Dean received 58 percent of the vote, enough to beat Kerry's 34, even though Dean had dropped out of the race nearly two weeks before. It was Dean's first victory in the primaries. "This win means so much to me," he said in a written statement. "While I ran for president, I often said America would be a better place if it was more like Vermont. I still firmly believe that to be true."

As Kerry was celebrating his success at his home in Georgetown, awaiting the moment when he could make his victory speech in the Post Office Square, he received telephone calls. At 7:30, a call came in from John Edwards, who had hoped to win in Ohio and Georgia and keep his campaign alive. With big losses from coast to coast, it was time for him to drop out of the race. He canceled plans to fly to Dallas, where he was going to campaign on Wednesday, and announced that he would return that night to Raleigh, North Carolina, so he could formally withdraw from the race the next day. In the call to Kerry, Edwards was upbeat. He said he wanted to sit down with Kerry soon to unite the party; then the two talked about how, to quote David Wade, they "rode out the tough times" on the campaign trail. At 8:00, a surprise call came in from George W. Bush, who was phoning Kerry to congratulate him on his victories. Bush told Kerry he had prevailed in a tough field. He also said he was looking forward to a "spirited" race in the fall. Kerry responded by saying he hoped "we have a great debate about the issues before the country." Then Kerry told Bush he remembered "seeing you up in New Hampshire in 2000. Now I understand the process you went through."

Later, when Kerry stepped onto the stage in the Post Office Square before a national television audience, as the crowd assembled before him cheered wildly, he did not back away from his attack on Bush, even though he had just spoken with him on the telephone. "Tonight," he began, "the message could not be clearer. All across our country, change is coming to America. Thank you to voters from coast to coast who have truly made this a Super Tuesday." He remembered how he had gotten where he was. "I particularly want to say thank you to the people of Iowa and New Hampshire, who gave me a hearing when no one thought we had a chance. And they sent us on our way." He had words of praise for John Edwards—"Edwards brings a compelling voice to our party, great eloquence to the cause of working men and women all across our nation and great promise for leadership for the years to come"—as well as for Howard Dean— his was an "unprecedented contribution."

But what excited the crowd most was his assault on Bush. "If George Bush wants to make national security the central issue in this campaign," Kerry said, "I have three words for him that I know he understands: Bring it on!" It was a line he had used often in the past; tonight, it got an even greater response. "George Bush," he said, "who promised to become a uniter, has become the great divider. He proposed to amend the Constitution of the United States for political purposes, and we say that he has no right to misuse the most precious document in our history in an effort to divide this nation and distract us from our goals. We resoundingly reject the politics of fear and distortion." Finally, Kerry laid out what he expected to happen in the upcoming campaign. "We have no illusions," he said, "about the Republican attack machine and what our opponents have done in the past and what they may try to do in the future. But I know that together, we are equal to this task."

THE CANDIDATE

On the day after Super Tuesday, Kerry had his party's nomination all but wrapped up. As a result, the overriding question was, whom would he select as his running mate? As if to underscore this fact, Kerry appointed the person who would run his vice-presidential search committee: Jim Johnson, a friend of his from Ketchum, Idaho, the resort town where Teresa owned a vacation home. A former adviser to Walter Mondale and a successful merchant banker, Johnson had once served as chairman and chief executive officer of Fannie Mae. At present, he worked with the Media Fund, a Democratic activist group. Kerry trusted Johnson to fulfill his mission using guidelines that Kerry set down: find the best possible candidate—a person who could become president, not just someone who could help him win—and do so in a manner as private and dignified as possible. Even now, Kerry was troubled by the way Al Gore had conducted his selection process before the media, especially since Kerry had been one of the three men who ended up on the short list and, as a result, the object of much of the media scrutiny.

Public speculation had already begun about a running mate for Kerry. While talking to reporters, Jennifer Palmieri, Edwards's press secretary, stated flatly that should Kerry approach Edwards, "I don't think he would say no." On CNN, Hillary Rodham Clinton took her name out of the running—almost. "That is totally up to the nominee," Clinton told Lou Dobbs. "I don't think I would be offered, and I don't think I would accept." (Clinton had become the master of advancing a story through denials.)

That same day, in Arlington, Virginia, the campaign to reelect George W. Bush unveiled its first television ads in order to draw attention away from Kerry, now that he was the presumed nominee. These initial ads were designed to create an affirmative, optimistic image of Bush. As it turned out, the ads got a lot more attention than the campaign had bargained for, since the ads used images from September 11th, which struck some as exploiting a national tragedy for political use and drew a firestorm of criticism.

One ad, "Safer, Stronger," showed firefighters carrying the flag-draped remains of a victim from the rubble of Ground Zero. Though the image appeared only briefly, it was shocking, especially to family members of the victims. The *New York Daily News* quoted Monica Gabrielle, whose husband had died on September 11th: "It's a slap in the face of the murder of 3,000 people." The paper then offered this from Kristen Breitweiser, who also lost her husband and was one of the activist widows who urged the formation of the 9/11 investigating commission: "After 3,000 people were murdered on his watch, it seems to me that it takes an awful lot of audacity. Honestly, it's in poor taste." More than the victims' family members were offended by the ads. Firefighters were angry too. Tommy Fee, a firefighter in

Rescue Squad 270 in Queens, told the *Daily News:* "It's as sick as people who stole things out of the place. The image of firefighters at Ground Zero should not be used for this stuff, for politics." Harold Schaitberger, president of the International Association of Firefighters, issued a statement: "Bush is calling on the biggest disaster in our country's history, and indeed in the history of the fire service, to win sympathy for his campaign." In its first week of advertising, the Bush campaign planned to spend $5 million on running ads in seventeen battleground states and on national cable television networks. No one in the campaign had imagined that the ad buy would produce bad publicity.

Meanwhile, in Raleigh, North Carolina, John Edwards, with his wife, Elizabeth, beside him, in the high school where two of his children had been students (one was Wade, his 16-year-old son who was killed in a car accident in 1996), announced that he was suspending his campaign. Arriving in the auditorium as the song "Take Me Home" played on the public-address system, Edwards began by saying, "Man, it is good to be home!" It had been a long road for him. After making millions as a successful malpractice and product-liability lawyer, Edwards, haunted by the tragic death of his son, had decided to go into politics. Elected to the Senate in 1998, he soon distinguished himself as one of the party's rising stars. He had announced his candidacy for president after New Year's Day in 2003, strolling down the driveway outside his home in Raleigh to break the news to reporters. For much of the next year, he languished in the polls, even after his official announcement in September in Robbins, North Carolina. Then, finally, in early January of 2004, he made his "two Americas" speech, which detailed his belief that in the United States there were two different countries, one for the rich and one for "everybody else." Once he embraced old-fashioned populism, Edwards caught on. The excitement propelled him to a second-place finish in Iowa, as former Dean supporters flocked to him when they decided they could not vote for Dean. But Edwards did badly in New Hampshire, harmed by Wesley Clark, and finished fourth behind Clark. He never fully recovered. In the end he won just South Carolina, the state where he was born. Now he was dropping out, but he made sure to do so in such a way as to position himself as a possible running mate for Kerry. "John Kerry," he said in his thirteen-minute speech, "has what it takes right here"—he pointed to his gut—"to be president of the United States. I will do everything I have in my power to help him."

On Thursday, Kerry focused on how his campaign and the Democratic Party would work together in the future. Since the Bush campaign had raised $144 million through January and intended to raise another $40 million before it stopped—the campaign had randomly picked $180 million as its goal, one it would eventually surpass—Kerry had to commit to a strategy that would enable him to raise enough money to compete. He announced that he planned to raise $80 million by midsummer. To do so, the campaign would bring to Washington a coterie of the party's top fund-raisers, and Kerry would embark on a twenty-city fund-raising tour intended to bring in another $20 million. Encouraged by the fact that he had raised $2 million over the Internet since Super Tuesday, Kerry intended to increase his efforts to bring in money online, perhaps inspired by the example of Howard Dean.

Because fund-raising was such a priority, Kerry decided not to replace Terry McAuliffe as chairman of the Democratic National Committee, even though Kerry had been upset with McAuliffe over the timing of his comments about Bush's National Guard experience.

(Kerry felt McAuliffe had brought up the issue too soon.) Still, more than anything, Kerry needed cash, and over the last decade McAuliffe had raised $500 million for Bill and Hillary Clinton's political endeavors. He was too valuable to lose; in fact, he had already raised $17.3 million that he was prepared to give to the Kerry campaign. Hillary Clinton underscored McAuliffe's importance when she said on the day Kerry announced his fund-raising plan, "A lot of plans have been laid, a lot of infrastructure put in place, and I want to see us follow through. Terry has helped the Democratic Party move into the twenty-first century to compete against the incredible interlocking institutional powers of the other side." To stay in place, McAuliffe had to assure the Kerry campaign that he would not make incendiary statements without clearing them with the campaign first. Mary Beth Cahill was diplomatic in her remarks. "He's prepared the troops of the Democratic Party," she said, "and we need his help to mobilize those troops and we're leaving him in place. . . . We don't have any further plans. . . . Just six weeks ago, we were dead."

As the Kerry campaign was firming up its future, the Bush campaign was dealing with the fallout from the ads with the images of September 11th. Karen Hughes, a special assistant to the president, who had long advised Bush on media matters, made a round of television talk-show appearances to defend Bush's commercials. "I think it's very tasteful," she told a reporter on CNN. "It's a reminder of our shared experience as a nation. I mean, September 11th is not just some distant tragedy from the past; it really defined our future." Maybe, but that afternoon, the firefighters union, which had supported Kerry during the primaries, called on Bush to stop airing the commercials. At the same time, the Kerry campaign sent out an e-mail blast to reporters that included a 2002 Associated Press article in which

Bush was quoted as saying, at a time when he was trying to get more funding out of Congress to deal with the aftermath of September 11th, "I have no ambition whatsoever to use this as a political issue."

By Friday, the White House was in full spin control. The use of the September 11th images had created a controversy that the Bush campaign had not anticipated. The situation got even worse when the White House announced that the next week Bush would attend the groundbreaking of a September 11th memorial to be built in Eisenhower Park on Long Island, New York, to commemorate Nassau County citizens who had died in the World Trade Center. If that were not problematic enough, what with the flurry of criticism being directed at Bush by the firefighters and the victims' families, the White House said that, three hours after the groundbreaking ceremony, Bush would attend a fund-raiser at the Carlton restaurant—also in Eisenhower Park—where he would collect $1 million. When spokesperson Stephanie Cutter weighed in on behalf of the Kerry campaign—"Is President Bush going to use the money that he raises on top of this 9/11 memorial to pay for his ads that make political hay out of that very tragic day?"—she politicized the situation. So, Scott McClellan, the White House press secretary, felt compelled to call a *New York Times* reporter in Crawford, Texas, where Bush was vacationing on his ranch, to explain why Bush was going to attend the two events so close together. "The president was invited," McClellan said, referring to the groundbreaking. "The president was honored to accept and pay tribute to those who lost their lives. September 11th is a day the president will never forget." Stating the obvious—who would ever forget September 11th?—did not mollify those who found the juxtaposed events upsetting and exploitative.

Following the adage that the best defense is a good offense, the Republican National Committee—that is to say, the Bush campaign—

chose Friday to launch an Internet boxing game called "Kerry versus Kerry." The GOP said that the game was meant to show Kerry's "multiple positions on multiple issues," and depicted one Kerry fighting another Kerry, underscoring the idea that he had often taken different positions on the same subject. This, according to the GOP, was an indication that Kerry would be an unsteady leader.

On Saturday, Bush announced that he had no intentions of pulling his ads using images from September 11th. Taking questions from reporters on his ranch, with President Vincente Fox of Mexico standing at his side, Bush said, "First of all, I will continue to speak about the effects of 9/11 on our country and my presidency. How this administration handled that day, as well as the war on terror, is worthy of discussion. And I look forward to discussing that with the American people. And I look forward to the debate about who is best to lead this country in the war on terror."

For his part, Kerry decided to attack Bush not on the use of the images of September 11th but on the economy. On Maverick Square in San Antonio, standing before a huge Lone Star flag, Kerry took direct aim at Bush. "I think George Bush ought to leave the ranch and come out and talk to people who've lost their jobs," he said. "I think he ought to leave the ranch and come out and talk to people who don't have any health care. He won't have any trouble finding them in Texas, because there are 5.6 million of them here in this state."

On Monday, Kerry made a statement that briefly redirected the political debate. At a breakfast fund-raiser in Florida, someone in the audience of fifty asked Kerry about Europeans who were "counting on us" to "get rid of Bush." In response, Kerry stated what many political observers felt was obvious: numerous foreign countries were unhappy with Bush. "I've met foreign leaders," Kerry said, "who can't go out and say this publicly, but, boy, they look at you and say, 'You gotta win this, you gotta beat this guy, we need a new policy,' things like that." A quick perusal of a variety of newspapers in European countries would seem to substantiate what Kerry said. Rarely has there been such a strong anti-American feeling throughout Europe, especially in such countries as France, Germany, Italy, and Spain. But the Bush brain trust decided to make an issue out of Kerry's statement, sending the vice president out to demand in a speech made in Arizona that Kerry release a list of the foreign leaders with whom he had spoken. Kerry refused.

On Wednesday, at his headquarters in Washington, Kerry met with Howard Dean. They posed together in the lobby—they hugged and shook hands—as members of Kerry's staff looked on and applauded, and then had an hour-long private meeting. Although he would not formally endorse Kerry—that would have to wait for another day—Dean released a statement after the meeting, saying, "During the campaign, we often focused on what divided us, but the truth is we have much more in common, beginning with our fervent desire to send George Bush back to Crawford, Texas, in November." Following the Dean head-to-head, Kerry met with Terry McAuliffe at the Democratic National Committee offices to discuss future strategy. In addition, John J. Sweeney, the president of the AFL-CIO, announced that his union was going to spend $44 million in the upcoming election to defeat Bush. "America's unions," he said, "are united for the biggest and earliest mobilization effort for the 2004 elections in the union movement's history."

But the news of the day occurred that morning in Chicago as Kerry greeted a group of factory workers following a speech. A boom mike from National Public Radio picked up Kerry's voice as he spoke to the workers. "These are the most crooked, you know, lying group I've ever seen," Kerry said. "It's scary." As soon as the comment was broadcast, the story was picked up by all media outlets. Here was the Democratic candidate for president calling a Republican group "crooked" and "lying," but exactly who was the group? Following the incident, Kerry refused to take questions from reporters. Instead, David Wade, who had become the spokesman who most accurately conveyed Kerry's true feelings, said that the group to which Kerry was referring was "the Republican attack machine," which had mislabeled him as a tax-and-spend liberal and was now accusing him of flip-flopping on issues. That day, the Republican National Committee demanded an apology from Kerry, with Marc Racicot, the RNC chairman, describing Kerry's comments as "unbecoming of a presidential candidate." Racicot said Kerry should "apologize for his negative attack." Kerry refused.

The following day, the Republicans in Congress tried to keep the controversy from dying when a group of legislators headed by Speaker of the House Dennis Hastert held a press conference on Capitol Hill. "I am one of those Republicans in Illinois," Hastert said at the press conference, even though there was no indication that Kerry had been referring to Illinois Republicans. "If he wants to describe me as being crooked and a liar, I think he will have his comeuppance coming." Then Rick Santorum, the Pennsylvania senator who sat in the seat once held by John Heinz, added that he felt Kerry's remark was "outside the bounds of where people who want to hold the highest office of this country . . . should be making." Kerry ignored the Republicans. Following a meeting with Democratic leaders on Capitol Hill, he spoke with reporters. "I have no intention whatsoever of apologizing for my remarks," he said. "I think the Republicans need to start talking about the real issues before this country. This is a Republican attack squad that specializes in trying to destroy people and be negative. I haven't said anything that's incorrect about them. They've said a lot of things that are incorrect." He cited the advertising and publicity campaigns waged by the Bush campaign against John McCain in the South Carolina primary in 2000 and by the Republican Party against Max Cleland in the Georgia Senate race in 2002—two races in which, Kerry believed, honorable veterans saw their military records and positions on national security distorted for the sake of politics.

As Republicans and Democrats dug in for a nasty and bitter eight-month endurance contest, tragic events unfolded in Europe with chilling and horrific ramifications. On Thursday morning, March 11, in Madrid, while people were making their way to work, ten explosions erupted on four crowded commuter trains. The first estimates said that 200 people had been killed and 1,500 wounded, making this the worst terrorist attack in modern Spanish history, and the international media began to describe the massacre as Spain's "September 11th." Prime Minister Jose Maria Aznar called the attack "mass murder." In the days that followed, it became clear that the attack—bombs had been placed on the trains in backpacks and detonated by remote control—was carried out by al Qaeda in an attempt to influence the pending elections in Spain.

On Friday, March 12, Kerry began running an ad, scheduled to air for one week in sixteen battleground states, that answered claims made by the Bush campaign that electing Kerry would result in a $900-billion tax increase—an assertion that was unsubstantiated within the ad. "Once again," the voice-over narrator says in Kerry's ad, "George Bush is misleading America. John Kerry has never called for a nine-hundred-billion-dollar tax increase. He wants to cut taxes for the middle class." Then, as a shot of the White House flashes across the screen, the narrator delivers the kicker. "Doesn't America deserve more from its president than misleading negative ads?"

On Sunday, the attacks against Kerry continued when Secretary of State Colin Powell appeared on *Fox News Sunday* to demand that Kerry release the list of names of world leaders who wanted him to defeat Bush. "If he feels it is that important an assertion to make," Powell said, "he ought to list some names. If he can't list names, then perhaps he should find something else to talk about." The timing was especially bad for Powell, since on that very day, in the elections being held in Spain, the ruling Popular Party was voted out of office for the Socialist Party in what was seen as a referendum on Spain's support of the war being waged by Bush in Iraq. Had Spain not had troops in Iraq, this line of reasoning said, al Qaeda would not have carried out its terrorist attack in Madrid three days earlier. The new prime minister, José Luis Rodriquez Zapatero, promptly announced that Spain would withdraw its troops from Iraq.

On Tuesday, Kerry won the Illinois primary, giving him 2,252 delegates—more than the 2,162 needed to secure the nomination. It was official: John Kerry was going to be his party's candidate for president.

With the nomination wrapped up, Kerry decided to take a few days off. On Wednesday night, he flew to Ketchum, Idaho, where he would spend time relaxing at the house on Big Wood River, owned by Teresa Heinz. Over the next five days, he rested as much as he could and went skiing or snowboarding every day. Not surprisingly, the media turned its attention to Kerry's performance on the slopes. One incident that merited massive press coverage occurred when a Secret Service agent accidently knocked Kerry down on the slopes on

Mount Brady and Kerry responded later by referring to the agent as "that sonofabitch."

On March 20, *The New York Times* ran an article on its front page entitled "90 Day Strategy by Bush's Aides to Define Kerry" which reported that the Bush campaign was going to paint Kerry as a man who would be indecisive and lacking in conviction as a leader. The plans for the attack, according to the article, had been made weeks ago by Karl Rove, Bush's campaign adviser. The goal was to define Kerry to a vast majority of the public by early June before he had time to raise money to start running his own ads. The assault had started in the previous week with ads suggesting that Kerry would raise taxes if elected and weaken the Patriot Act. Next, the article said, the Bush campaign would portray Kerry as "weak on defense." "The problem with that front-page article in the *Times*," one well-placed Republican insider says, "is this: if you are truly confident about your plan of attack, you don't publish the details of that plan on the front page of *The New York Times*. That's just plain stupid. Now everyone—the public, your opponent—knows what you're going to do."

For their part, the Kerry inner circle had made the point of studying past campaigns, especially those of McCain and Gore, to see how to run against Rove, whom one senior Kerry staffer described this way: "We have respect for his political acumen but contempt for his morality because he'll do anything to win, including putting this country in a war in a very political way." From the Gore campaign, as one Kerry adviser says, "We learned that we must use every weapon available to the Democratic Party, which Gore, who muzzled Bill Clinton, did not do. If that means using Clinton in some states, we'll do it. If that means using Ted Kennedy in some states, we'll do it."

From the Bush-McCain race, the Kerry campaign derived an equally important lesson. "You have to hit these guys back when they slime you," David McKean says. "In the spring and early summer, they tried with the veterans issues, the military service, and we responded at every point in a very harsh manner. It's hard to know where they'll go in the fall. Anything negative about John Kerry is out there. There is nothing new. But these retread stories can get traction. There will be lots of them, and we'll be ready for them."

On March 21, Richard C. Clarke, the former counterterrorism adviser for the National Security Agency, appeared on *60 Minutes* to announce the publication of his book *Against All Enemies: Inside America's War on Terror,* which revealed that from the time he took office in January of 2001 until September 11th, Bush did not take the issue of terrorism seriously, even going so far as to ignore reports that warned of the possibility of an attack on the American soil. Clarke followed his pre-publication publicity spree with an appearance before the 9/11 Commission, which had been formed to investigate the causes of September 11th—testimony that proved to be as explosive as promised. The combination of the publication of *Against All Enemies* (which became an instant number-one best seller nationwide) and the media coverage afforded Clarke, the terrorist attacks in Spain, and recent comments made by the president of Poland ("That they deceived us about the weapons of mass destruction, that's true. We were taken for a ride.") called into question the full spectrum of what had come to be known as the Bush Doctrine. Judging from recent events, it did not seem reasonable that Bush would base his campaign for reelection on his handling of foreign policy—on the contrary, it seemed that Bush's handling of foreign policy had been profoundly misguided—but that was precisely what he was doing.

On the evening of Thursday, March 25, the Democratic National Committee held a fund-raiser in Washington called the Unity Dinner. Featuring appearances by President Jimmy Carter, President Bill Clinton, Vice President Al Gore, John Kerry, and the candidates who had run against Kerry in the primaries, the purpose of the dinner was to raise money—the 2,000 people who attended gladly ate their barbecue dinner off plastic plates to spend as little of the $11 million raised that night as possible—and to show the Republicans that Kerry would be running in the fall with the party solidly behind him. In the best speech of the night, Bill Clinton put the Bush inner circle on notice, scoffing, "They remind me of teenagers who got their inheritance too soon and couldn't wait to blow it."

Kerry was the last to speak. "Above all," he said, "this country of ours, which we love, deserves leadership that faces the truth and tells the truth—that trusts the American people and knows that when we live up to our values, the United States of America never goes to war because it wants to—we only go to war because we have to."

Earlier in the day, Dean endorsed Kerry at an event at George Washington University. Kerry also received the endorsement of the United Auto Workers and the American Federation of State, County, and Municipal Employees, whose president, Gerald W. McEntee, pledged to spend $30 million to defeat Bush.

With his campaign going strong, on March 31, Kerry was admitted into Massachusetts General Hospital in Boston to have surgery to repair tears in two tendons in his rotator cuff. An old injury caused by a bicycle accident had been aggravated in January when his campaign bus had stopped abruptly in Iowa. Upon his release later that day, his physician, Bertram Zarins, the team doctor for the New

England Patriots, the Boston Bruins, and the New England Revolution soccer team, pronounced the surgery a success, adding that, except for not shaking hands for two weeks, Kerry could resume a normal routine.

I n the first week of April, Kerry made appearances in which he depicted himself as a fiscal conservative. On April 3, Kerry released a report arguing that Bush was running up the deficit and damaging state budgets with his out-of-control federal spending. It was Kerry's attempt to represent Bush as a "don't-tax-but-spend-anyway," fiscally irresponsible budget-buster. It was a designation made even more relevant by the fact that Kerry had supported much of the tax policy promoted by Ronald Reagan.

Four days later, at George Washington University, Kerry gave a major economic address in which he argued that it was necessary to have "pay as you go" spending in Congress. When Clinton had left office in January of 2001, the Congressional Budget Office, which is politically unbiased, said there would be a $5-trillion future surplus; now, at the beginning of the fourth year of the Bush Administration, there was a projected $4 trillion deficit. "When I say a cap on spending," Kerry said, "I mean it." Combined with an economic address he had given last month in Detroit, the speech helped shore up Kerry's credentials as a deficit hawk. On April 8, *The New York Times* ran an editorial called "John Kerry, Fiscal Conservative." In it, the paper said: "Yesterday at Georgetown University, Senator John Kerry delivered a forceful speech on the virtues of responsible budgeting. On top of his recent nuanced proposals on corporate taxes, Mr. Kerry's performance suggests he is starting to hit his stride in thinking and talking about the economy. . . . The Kerry speech was a call for a return to the Clinton Administration's emphasis on cutting the deficit and public debt as a means of instilling confidence in the American economy."

This week also saw the last fund-raiser held—on April 5—by the Bush campaign. After fifty-five fund-raisers in thirty-two states, the campaign had raised $180 million. For his part, Kerry had raised $79 million so far, $50 million of it in the last three months. Half of the $50 million had come in over the Internet. As the money was flooding in—to both campaigns—Kerry was making changes on his staff. He named John Sasso as the general election chairman of the Democratic National Committee, in effect his representative on the committee that runs the Democratic Party.

There was also a shake-up in the Kerry inner circle. As the campaign prepared to make a huge ad buy to counteract the Bush assault, there had been a disagreement between Robert Shrum and Jim Margolis, the two men responsible for creating and producing Kerry's political ads in the primaries, over how the ad commission would be split. The campaign did not want to pay a standard commission, which can sometimes be 10 to 15 percent of the amount of the ad buy. Mary Beth Cahill told Shrum and Margolis to decide how much commission they would charge and how it would be split between them. In reality, the commission would be paid to the company that each man represented—Shrum, Devine, & Donilon for Shrum, GMMB for Margolis. When Shrum and Margolis could not work out an agreement, Cahill intervened, but not enough to resolve the conflict. Shrum wanted a larger cut of the commission—a proposal Margolis would not accept. Finally, when it became clear that their differences could not be resolved, Margolis walked away, telling the press he would play a reduced role in the campaign. As he had before, Shrum won out, securing his position as the principal media adviser for the Kerry campaign.

On April 10, Kerry went after Bush on his handling of foreign policy. Saying that the situation in Iraq was hopelessly chaotic because the Bush Administration was "gridlocked by its own ideology and its own arrogance," Kerry told a television reporter in Chicago that he would be able to handle foreign policy better than Bush had done. "I think you measure leadership by the lifetime of experience," Kerry said. "And I bring more experience in military affairs, foreign policy, and national affairs than George Bush even has today, more experience. George Bush, in my judgment, has run a foreign policy that has made us less safe than we ought to be in the aftermath of 9/11." Four days later, almost as an answer to Kerry's claims of military leadership, *The Boston Globe* ran a story in which Grant Hibbard, one of Kerry's commanding officers in Vietnam, said that Kerry didn't deserve the first Purple Heart he was awarded. On the day that the *Globe* story appeared, Hibbard told the *New York Post*: "There was just a little scratch on his forearm and he was holding a small piece of shrapnel. It didn't look like much of a wound to me. I didn't think he deserved a Purple Heart."

This controversy did not disrupt Kerry's fund-raising momentum. On the evening of April 13, he held a fund-raiser attended by 3,300 people at the Sheraton Hotel in Boston, where he brought in $5 million—$4 million for his campaign and $1 million for the DNC—which made it the largest fund-raiser in Massachusetts history. In his remarks, Kerry addressed the issue of what it means to be a conservative: "There is nothing conservative, whatsoever, about this administration, which has taken surpluses as far as the eye can see and turned them into deficits as far as the eye can see. . . . There is nothing conservative about an attorney general who disrespects the Constitution and steps on the civil rights and civil liberties of Americans. And there is nothing conservative about a president of the United States who toys with the greatest document in political history, the Constitution of the United States, during an election year for political purposes to drive a wedge between the American people."

The next night, Kerry held a fund-raiser at the Sheraton Hotel in New York City. At that event, he raised a staggering $6.5 million, easily making it the largest fund-raiser ever held in the state of New York. (George Bush had brought in $4.8 million at a similar fund-raiser in June.) That night, Kerry could not help but joke, "Why do they call George Bush 43? Now I understand—it's his approval rating."

On April 15, the Bush campaign began airing another attack ad, this one calling into question Kerry's commitment to U.S. troops in Iraq because he had voted against Bush's $87-billion appropriations bill. This ad infuriated Kerry more than any that the Bush campaign had aired so far. In Pittsburgh, before an audience of 10,000 at the University of Pittsburgh, Kerry went after the Bush inner circle, focusing on Dick Cheney and Karl Rove. "I'm tired of Karl Rove and Dick Cheney and a bunch of people who went out of their way to avoid their chance to serve when they had the chance," Kerry said, standing before a giant American flag. (Both Cheney and Rove had used deferments to stay out of the military during the Vietnam War.) "I'm not going to listen to them talk to me about patriotism. I've seen how these people in the White House today, in their twisted sense of ethics and morality, don't think twice about challenging John McCain and what happened to him as a prisoner of war."

On Sunday, when Kerry appeared on *Meet the Press*, Tim Russert asked him about the rhetoric he had used in the speeches he had made as a member of the antiwar movement in the early 1970s. "If you wanted to ask me, 'Have you ever made mistakes in your life,' sure," Kerry said. "I think some of the language that I used was a language that reflected an anger." It was what the press would describe as a "near-apology." When Russert played clips from Kerry's testimony before the Senate Foreign Relations Committee, Kerry was especially sensitive. "The words were honest," he said, "but, on the other hand, they were a little over the top." In the interview, Russert also brought up recent charges made by the right wing that Kerry might have distorted his military record. To this, Kerry said he would release his military record to end any speculation.

By mid-April, the Bush campaign had spent $99 million, much of it on televison advertising, and the opinion polls showed the race as a dead heat, with Kerry slightly ahead in some polls and Bush ahead by an equally thin margin in others. Then again, the one lesson proven by the 2004 Democratic primary process was that the voter should not trust opinion polls or the media's reporting of opinion polls. It was far too soon to make predictions. Conventional wisdom had it that presidential elections were won or lost in October, not April.

On Wednesday, Kerry made good on his promise to release his military records when he posted his 140-page file on his Web site. The material answered Kerry's critics. First, it established that Kerry had volunteered to go to the war zone in Vietnam. "I consider the opportunity to serve in Vietnam," he had written on February 10, 1968, "an extremely important part of being in the armed forces and believe that my request is in the best interests of the navy." It documented evaluations made by his commanding officers during his first tour of duty when he was stationed on the *Gridley*. One commander said he was "intelligent, mature and rich in educational background and experience." He was also "polished, tactful, and outgoing," the officer said, and "a brilliant conversationalist. . . . He uses the English language expertly, both orally and in writing." Months later, a different commander stated: "His division's morale is one of the best on the ship due to his dynamic leadership. He is a polished diplomat at ease in distinguished company" and "is impressive in appearance and always immaculate."

Kerry also got glowing evaluations on his second tour, when he was "in country." George M. Elliott, his commander in early 1969, wrote this: "In a combat environment often requiring independent, decisive action, Lt. j.g. Kerry was unsurpassed. . . . His bearing and appearance are above reproach." On January 28, 1969, Lieutenant Commander Elliott wrote: "Involved in several enemy-initiated fire fights, including an ambush during the Christmas truce, he effectively suppressed enemy fire and is unofficially credited with 20 enemy killed in action." Even Grant Hibbard, who had raised doubts that Kerry deserved his first Purple Heart, had had nothing negative to say about Kerry two weeks after the actual incident. In a 16-point evaluation, Hibbard checked "not observed" in 12 categories, "one of the top few" in three categories, and "above the majority" in military bearing.

On April 27, on a bus ride between Youngstown and Cleveland, Kerry addressed the issue of military service—his own and that of members of the Bush Administration—with a reporter from the *Dayton Daily News*. "I think," he warned, "a lot of veterans are going to be very angry at a president who can't account for his own service in the National Guard, and a vice president who got every deferment in the world and decided he had better things to do, criticizing somebody who fought for their country and served." The issue was revisited the next day, when Senator Frank Lautenberg of New Jersey attacked members of the Bush Administration on the floor of the Senate, saying, "We know who the chicken hawks are. They talk tough on national defense and military issues and cast aspersions on others, but when it was their turn to serve, they were AWOL from courage."

In the coming weeks, events unfolded that had an effect on the presidential race as it was developing. The prison abuse scandal in Iraq underscored the fact that the war there, as it was being conducted by the Bush Administration, was veering out of control. For the first time, Bush's handling of the war in Iraq was having a severely negative impact on his approval rating.

On the domestic front, the candidacy of Ralph Nader, so vital to the results of the race in 2000, was also noteworthy. Knowing Nader could influence the fall campaign, Kerry made a point to meet with him in Washington on May 19 to discuss a variety of topics, among them the presidential election. Simply by meeting with Nader, Kerry was handling the situation differently than Gore, who refused even to return Nader's phone calls—a snub, many believe, that may have cost Gore the election since, under the right circumstances, Nader might have been convinced to drop out of the race. On the contrary, following their meeting, Nader told a reporter Kerry and he had agreed to keep the "communication lines open."

"John Kerry and Ralph Nader have a relationship going back thirty years," Mary Beth Cahill says, "to the environmental movement and the consumer movement in the 1970s. They know each other, they know what they have in common, and they know where their differences lie. Their meeting was professional and thoughtful. I really believe that this year is different than 2000."

In general, as the weeks passed, the Kerry campaign began looking to the national political conventions and, beyond that, to the fall campaign. One upcoming area of concern was the debates. "Kerry is a smart, fierce debater," Cahill says. "He'll be ready for the fall debates against George Bush, who is also a strong debater. Bush wants the public to underestimate him." To prepare for these debates, according to a senior adviser, Kerry will have a research staff compile extensive memorandums to be mastered by him. A former Harvard debate champion, Bob Shrum will assemble a list of probable questions. Finally, Kerry will engage in a series of mock debates, with stand-ins playing Bush, the moderator, and the questioners.

If there was one chief concern for Kerry going forward from the conventions to the fall campaign, it was the money the Bush organization would be able to raise and spend. "Our biggest challenge will be the race against George Bush's Rangers and Pioneers," one Kerry staffer says, "We know that no Democrat can match Bush's special interest war chest dollar for dollar."

Over Memorial Day weekend, as he went about campaigning, John Kerry answered questions posed to him by a journalist via text-messaging e-mail.

"How will you prepare to debate Bush?"

"George Bush is a worthy adversary," Kerry wrote, "and I want our debates to be a fight for the truth, not a food fight. I just hope the president will embrace the spirit of real debates in our democracy. You'd think the president would want to debate the issues once a month for the course of this campaign instead of cheating the country with nothing but attack ads on TV."

"How will you handle being attacked by the Bush campaign?"

"I know something about fighting for myself, and I have a band of brothers who stick up for each other when the chips are down. I don't let their attacks silence me or scare me. I've been through a lot worse."

"What lessons did you learn from the Gore campaign, from the Bush-McCain race in 2000?"

"I learned you have to fight back with the truth right away. These guys are ruthless. They'll say and do anything. If they could do what they did to John McCain and Max Cleland and still live with themselves, then I don't put anything past them."

"Do you have a political guru?"

"Hell, no," Kerry wrote. "People are electing a president, not a political advisor or a pundit. We saw what happens when a candidate for president says, 'Look at this great team. They'll take care of everything.' "

"What will be your hardest challenge between August and November?"

"We have a fight on our hands," Kerry wrote. "They're going to have unlimited money, and they're going to pull every lever they can to game the system. We just have to stand up for ourselves against their money and their bareknuckle politics."

In early June, a memo circulated among senior Kerry staff. Entitled "Fighting Back, Staying Strong: A Seven-Point Roadmap to Victory in November," it contained information suggesting it was written by an adviser to the campaign, based in New York, though not a staffer. It implored them to ignore the doubters, "the same people who said Gov. Bill Clinton was dead going into the Democratic Convention in third place behind a crazy Texas billionaire and a guy named Bush who didn't know what a grocery scanner was for. As we head into the home stretch before the convention," the memo read, "let's all keep the following points in mind":

"1. Accentuate John Kerry's strengths as a candidate. He's the message, you're the messengers. Remember that John Kerry has exhibited as much presidential leadership as any guy since Eisenhower and John Kennedy ran for president. Always accentuate his assets. Vietnam veteran. Former prosecutor. Highly successful senator now serving in his fourth term. On fiscal issues, he's a hawk. On social issues, he's a sensible progressive. On national security and foreign policy, he's experienced—he's been in the military and he's dealt with foreign policy hands-on in the Senate. On the personal front, he's a good father, stepfather, and husband. In other words, he's got it all, and that should be our overriding message. People still have serious doubts about the other guy's capacity to do the job in a dangerous world.

"2. Bush's Record. We should always highlight the fact that Bush is a failed president. First president since Hoover to lose jobs on his watch—a failed leader on the economy. The environment in decay—a failed leader on environmental issues. The war in Iraq overly ideological and horribly planned—a failed military leader. The terrorists at bay (witness the attacks in Spain and Osama bin Laden getting away at Tora Bora)—a failed leader in the war on terror. Remember Ronald Reagan's line 'Are you better off than you were four years ago?' Today, following 9/11, one could ask, 'Are you as safe as [Bush] said you'd be?' Most people would probably answer no, and Bush's failure as a leader in the war on terror is responsible for that fact.

"3. The Military Record. Remember that while John Kerry is a decorated Vietnam veteran, Bush does not have a comparable record to run on. There are lingering questions about his conduct in the National Guard, but then there is the larger question. He wants to be seen as a 'war' president, yet he does not have a military record to justify that title. Nor do the people around him. You've got Dick Cheney and his deferments, Paul Wolfowitz and his chickenhawks, and let's not forget Rove. At a time when John Kerry was in the navy in the late sixties, Rove was hopping from one university to another—holding on to the deferment he needed to keep him out of Vietnam—and this is the guy who devised attacks on the service of McCain and Cleland?

"4. Hit back as hard as they hit us. Or harder. Here is the lesson we must learn from the Michael Dukkakis campaign in 1988, the John McCain campaign in 2000, and the Al Gore campaign in 2000: When we get hit by the other side, we hit back as hard or harder. We can never allow their lies to go unanswered. Our goal should be to answer the lie, whatever it is, within the news cycle. I'm tired of namby pamby pimply Harvard educated pasty Democrats who'd rather be whiners than winners, always cringing and asking 'What are we gonna do when Karl Rove attacks us?' How about somebody asking what they're gonna do when we hold them accountable for what they've done on the issues and for their sleazy tactics?

"5. Teresa Heinz Kerry. What we have learned so far is that the more people see of Teresa Heinz Kerry the more they like her. This is true especially of women. Let's make sure we play up THK's assets as a potential first lady. She's intelligent, savvy, truthful, and the best damn thing her husband has going for him. In the history of first ladies, she will be unique, with her impressive credentials as an accomplished philanthropist. But she's more than that—she's an authentic, truth-telling human being, an icon in Pennsylvania, a state Karl Rove covets, and she can bridge the divide between Democrats and the moderate Republicans John Kerry can turn into 'Kerry Republicans' the way Ronald Reagan converted 'Reagan Democrats.'

"6. It's still the economy, stupid. The other side is going to try to claim the economy is on the rebound. But we must stress the facts:

George Bush is the first president since Herbert Hoover to lose jobs. We have a wage recession. Local and state taxes are up. College tuition is rising. Health care costs are surging for families and businesses. History is on our side here. No president has been reelected with a net job loss. Note: with these recent good numbers on job growth, check to see if the jobs are mostly being created in battleground states and if they are connected to the federal government in one way or the other.

"7. John Kerry's Rose Garden Strategy. Lee Atwater used to way, 'When your enemy is shooting himself in the foot, stay out of the way, or you'll get hit by the bullets.' We know the Democratic base wants us to be as vocal as possible, but on some issues—the prison abuse in Iraq, for example—John Kerry is right to be himself: presidential. A guy capable of healing the country. If that means developing a bit of a rose garden strategy of our own in some cases, that will benefit us in the long run. We should never let them hit us without hitting back, but when Bush has gotten himself in a heap of trouble, when he's in the briar patch, stay out of the way.

"At this point in his presidency, Bush 41 was vulnerable. Bush 43 is in even more trouble. On the other hand, Kerry is solid, electable. If we follow our plan of attack, we can realize our goal of a victory in November."

By the time of the Democratic National Convention, held in Boston, in late July 2004, John Kerry had entered into history. Should he win, he would be only the 44th president. As such, as the primary season came to an end and the fall race loomed, there was an echo chamber of voices who held opinions about Kerry and the election. Mary Beth Cahill: "This is a perfect match of the man and the times. This is a moment in our nation's history when there is enormous uncertainty about our common security, about our place in the world. These are things that John Kerry discusses and thinks about with enormous fluency. Because of his life experiences, John Kerry is ready to lead, and he has proven that. His crewmates and friends testify to that fact. I think that that is a very big part of his appeal to voters." Max Cleland: "John Kerry went to Vietnam, won a Silver Star, went into combat, and came out as a bona fide, legitimate leader and hero. He also had the guts and courage to blow the whistle on a situation that was going south fast. As a Vietnam veteran, I respect both sides of that. I honor both sides of that. I guess you have to be a Vietnam veteran to understand." Teresa Heinz Kerry: "I think John is a better person when he's challenged because, looking at Vietnam and post-Vietnam, he can lead in those moments. He measures up to the challenge. I think a lot of people want to but can't. I also think he's a good debater—I know because I debate him all the time. He also has a very good gift of language. I think the feelings of measuring up to the moment, believing and being able to communicate that, are very good assets. He also has a high standard of moral conduct for the country, for everyone, for himself." George Shipley, Democratic strategist: "Actually, this is Kerry's race to lose. Bush has a 44-percent negative. An incumbent's race is a referendum on the record of the incumbent. We have the empirical reality here of the greatest deficits in the history of the country. We have a stock market which is only inflated by a weak dollar. We have Bush uniting the world, the Muslim world, as no one has in history—in history!—since the time of the Second Crusade. The Democrats are as angry at him as the Republicans were at Clinton. The Democrat vote will be out, and Bush has no hope of being bipartisan. He has pandered to the religious right, and he has pandered to the far right in Israel.

And the Iraqi War— it's a political disaster." Sidney Blumenthal: "In 2000, Al Gore was told he was unlikable. Bush was seen as more likable. Gore tried to 'fix' his personality. People have many things to say about John Kerry's personality. But my view is, he should do nothing to fix it. He should simply campaign strongly and understand that character is not some abstraction that comes out of a poll. Character is action, and his character will be revealed in the action of his campaign. The worst mistake he could make is to repeat the error Gore made. Don't try to fix yourself. Your character will be revealed through your actions and decisions in the campaign."

ACKNOWLEDGMENTS

For their time, information, or support in the writing of this book, I would like to thank Adam Abrams, David Alston, Gita Amar, Christine Anderson, Dan Barbiero, Sidney Blumenthal, Douglas Brinkley, Tony Broccolo, Matt Butler, Mary Beth Cahill, Chad Clanton, Senator Max Cleland, Craig Crawford, Dan Crawford, Stephanie Crawford, Monica Crowley, Eugene Corey (of Brave New Words), Stephanie Cutter, Patricia Duff, Lars Erikson, Frank Gannon, Betsy Gotbaum, Edward W. Hayes, Susie Gilder Hayes, Christopher Heinz, George Hiltzik, Chris Jackson, Richard Johnson, Peggy Kerry, Teresa Heinz Kerry, Jeff Lewis, Jim Loftus, Mike McHaney, David McKean, Michael Medeiros, Michael Meehan, Lewis Miranda, Marvin Nicholson, Jennifer Palmieri, Jennifer Psaki, Julie Rassmann, James Rassmann, Iris Rossi, Del Sandusky, Ellen Sandusky, Pat Shearns, Richard Shepard, George Shipley, Michael Steinhardt, Roger Stone, Betty Thorson, Gene Thorson, Angelica

Torn, David Wade, Daniel White, Jamie Whitehead, Partrick Woodson.

In April of 2002, I published in *Rolling Stone* "Ready For His Close-Up," the first presidential profile of John Kerry. I would like to thank, at the magazine, Will Dana, Erika Fortgang Casriel, and Jann Wenner, and, for interviews for that article, Congressman Adam Smith, Senator Max Cleland, Senator John McCain, and Senator Edward M. Kennedy.

At Riverhead Books and The Penguin Group, I would like to thank Alex Morris and Susan Petersen Kennedy, but mostly Julie Grau, who is, quite simply, one of the best editors working in the publishing industry today.

ABOUT THE AUTHOR

PAUL ALEXANDER is a former reporter for *Time* magazine and has written for *Rolling Stone, The New York Times Magazine, The Nation, New York, The Village Voice,* and *The Guardian.* Alexander is the author of *Man of the People: The Life of John McCain* (2002) as well as biographies of Sylvia Plath, J. D. Salinger, and James Dean. Until recently, he was the co-host of *Batchelor & Alexander,* a nationally syndicated talk show on the ABC radio network. Alexander has also directed a documentary on Kerry's Vietnam years, entitled *Brothers in Arms.* He lives in New York City.